Eyewitness Accounts of the American Revolution

Journal of Events in the Revolution

Elias Boudinot

The New York Times & Arno Press

JOURNAL

OR

HISTORICAL RECOLLECTIONS

OF

AMERICAN EVENTS

DURING

THE REVOLUTIONARY WAR

BY

ELIAS BOUDINOT

President of the Continental Congress, Commissary General
of Prisoners in the Army of America during the Revolutionary War, Director of the Mint, etc.

Copied from His Own Original Manuscript.

PHILADELPHIA

FREDERICK BOURQUIN

1894

Edition limited to 315 copies,
of which
25 are large-paper quarto
290 are royal octavo.

This copy is Number

E. J. BICKING
PRINTER
TENTH AND MARKET STS
PHILADELPHIA.

REMARKS.

THIS Journal or Diary of Events which occurred during our Revolutionary War, is published, *verbatim, literatim et punctuatim,* from a faithful copy, made in 1874, of the original Journal written by Elias Boudinot, and which was then in the possession of Joseph J. Mickley, of Philadelphia. That the publication of the same is merely carrying out the desire of the author, who wished to bequeath to posterity a true and ungarbled account of the important occurrences of those times, is attested to by himself, in the early pages of the Journal; as he says, "A great many interesting anecdotes, that happened during the American Revolutionary War, are likely to be lost to posterity, by the negligence of the parties concerned, in not recording them. . . . . . I shall therefore without any attention to order, ... set down those I have had any acquaintance with, attending principally to the truth of the facts." Consequently, we have here a gathering of anecdotes of vital historical interest, bequeathed to us by him who participated in many of the occurrences, or which were narrated to him, at the time of their inception, by other participants.

Many of the narratives impart information not
to be obtained from any other source, while some
establish the claim to truthfulness of deeds which
were ascribed to individuals, and which have been,
until this publication, considered vague and imag-
inary; as instance the anecdote of John Aitken,
alias John the Painter, who intended to assassinate George the Third, but who was diverted from
the deed by Silas Deane, and destroyed instead
the naval stores at Portsmouth, England; also the
anecdote of the heroine, Lydia Darrah, who conveyed to the author the information of the intended
movements of the British Army at Philadelphia,
and the imparting of which to General Washington, saved the Continental Army a disastrous
defeat.

Here also will be found full accounts of the
exchange of General Charles Lee, who was captured by the British, and the indecent and per-
fidious manner in which he acted towards Washington immediately after; The capture of Major
Andre, and mention of his real captor, whom history has failed to name; *the poor old horse,* who
took the Tarrytown road, instead of the road to
New York; had he taken the latter, who can say
what would have been the outcome; The exposure
of the claim of Beaumarchais against the Continental Congress; The capture of Yorktown, and
Washington's expedient which led to the capitulation; Motion made in Congress to execute Lord

Cornwallis in retaliation for the murder of Colonel
Haines, as well as many other interesting narratives.

Throughout the whole Journal, the author is
laudatory of the character of his beloved chief,
Washington, and contributes, in no small way,
items of the greatest interest, gleaned through
personal intercourse with *the greatest of men*, ex-
tolling his ability as a General, his knowledge as a
Statesman, and his self-sacrifice as a Patriot; the
latter especially when the author approached him
with the view of resigning his commission as Commissary for the exchange of prisoners, on account
of Congress neglecting to supply him with money
to alleviate the sufferings of the prisoners in the
hands of the British at New York. To use the
author's own words, " In much distress & with
tears in his eyes, he assured me that if he was
deserted by the gentlemen of the country, he should
despair, He could not do everything, he was General, Quartermaster, and Commissary. Everything
fell on him and he was unequal to the task, he gave
me the most positive engagement that if I would
contrive any mode for their support and comfort,
he would confirm it as far as was in his power. On
this I told him that I knew of but one way and
that was to borrow money on my own private
security. He assured me that in case I did, and
was not reimbursed by Congress, he would go an
Equal sharer with me in the loss." Was ever

more patriotism or self-sacrifice exhibited, or more sympathy expressed for his fellow soldiers by any general, at any time, than by Washington in this instance.

The Diary terminates with a beautiful account of General Washington's passage from Elizabeth-Town, New Jersey, to New York, with the Committee of Congress, when first chosen President of the United States, 23d April, 1789.

Elias Boudinot was born in Philadelphia, May 2, 1740, and died in Burlington, New Jersey, October 24, 1821. He was appointed Commissary-General of Prisoners in the Army of America in 1777, and was elected a delegate to Congress from New Jersey, serving from 1778 till 1779, and again from 1781 to 1784. He was chosen President of Congress on November 4, 1782, and in that official capacity, signed the Treaty of Peace with England. In 1795 he was appointed by Washington, to succeed David Rittenhouse, as Director of the Mint, and held the office till July, 1805.

CONTENTS.

JOURNAL.

Copy of the Alarm sent by the Committee of Watertown, near Boston, to raise the Country. Rec'd by me as Chairman of the Committee of Safety at Elizabeth Town, in the Evening of 23rd April, 1775—

" WEDNESDAY MORNING near 11 o'clock.

WATER TOWN.

To all friends of American Liberty, be it known, that this morning before break of day, a Brigade, consisting of about 1000 or 1200 men, landed at Phipp's Farm at Cambridge and marched to Lexington, where they found a Company of our Militia in Arms, upon whom they fired without any provocation and killed 6 Men and Wounded 4 others.—By an Express from Boston we find another Brigade are now upon their march from Boston supposed to be about 1000—the Bearer Israel Bissel is charged to alarm the Country quite to Connecticut, and all Persons are desired to furnish him with fresh Horses, as they may be needed—I have spoken with several who have seen the dead and wounded.

J PALMER one of the Committee of S——y.

forwarded from Worcester April 19th 1775.

Brooklyn Thursday		11 o'clock.
Norwich	———	4 o'clock.
New London	———	7 o'clock.
Lynne	Friday morning	1 o'clock.
Say Brook	———	4 o'clock.
Shillingsworth	———	7 o'clock.
E Guilford	———	8 o'clock.
Guilford	———	10 o'clock.
Bradford	———	12 o'clock.
New Haven	———	April 21st.

rec'd & forwarded on certain Intelligence.

fairfield ——— April 22nd 8 o'clock.

THURSDAY 3 o'clock Afternoon.

Since the above rec'd the following by second Express.

Sir

I am this moment informed by Express from Woodstock, taken from the mouth of the Express that arrived there 2 o'clock Afternoon, that the

Contest between the first Brigade that marched to Concord, was still continuing this Morning at the Town of Lexington, to which Bridage had retreated.

That another Brigade said to be the Second, mentioned in the letter of this morning had landed with a quantity of Artillery, at the place where the first did.—The Provincials where determined to prevent the two Brigades from joining their strength if possible, and remain in great need of succor.

— N. B.   The Regulars when in Concord, burnt the Court House, took 2 pieces of Cannon, which they rendered useless and began to take up Concord Bridge, on which Capt. —— (who with many on both sides were soon killed) made an attack on the King's Troops, when they retreated to Lexington—

I am Sir
EB WILLIAMS

COL OBADIAH JOHNSON, Canterbury."

P. S.   Mr McFarland of Plainfield Mass., has just returned from Boston by way of Providence, who conversed with an Express from Lexington, who further informs, that about 4000 of our Troops had surrounded the first Brigade who were on a Hill in Lexington.   That the Action continued and there were about 50 of our men killed and 150 Regulars as near as they could determine when the Express came away—It will be expedient for every man to go, who is fit and willing.

NEW YORK COMMITTEE CHAMBER, 4 o'clock,
23rd April 1775 P.M.

Rec'd the within by Express & for'd by Express to N Brunswick with directions to stop at Elizabeth Town and acquaint the Committee there with the foregoing particulars   by order

J LOW

The Committee at New Brunswick are   Chairman
ordered to forward this to Philadelphia.

A great many interesting anecdotes, that happened during the American Revolutionary War, are likely to be lost to Posterity, by the negligence of the parties concerned, in not recording them, so that in future time they may be resorted to, as throwing great light on the eventful Crisis, of this important Æra—I shall therefore without any

attention to order, but merely as they arise in my
memory, set down those I have had any acquaintance with, attending principally to the TRUTH of
the facts.———

I was among the first of the citizens of New
Jersey who exerted ourselves in opposition to the
unconstitutional Acts of Great Britain then the
mother Country, and to whom the Citizens of
America were bound by the strongest habits of
filial affection and religious obedience. Nothing
was farther from our ideas, than a state of independence, on the Country from which we drew all our
Principles of Happiness and Enjoyment.

I had read an excellent treatise, said to have been
written by Lord Kaim, which in a very extraordinary
manner foretold the certainity of American Independence, in some future day, and that founded on
a train of solid reasoning, but we talked of it and
treated it as the generality of People now do the
accounts they read of the Millinium—

In 1775 I was chosen a Member of the provincial
Congress of New Jersey ; and when a proposition
was made by a few weak and Violent Men, for
raising a regiment of Troop, it was opposed by all the
Men of Note and understanding as a measure wholly
against our Duty and Allegiance to Great Britain
and rejected as contrary to every sentiment or
desire of our Constituents. A few week violent
Men (particularly a Wm. Smith, of Woodbridge)
were not only for raising a regiment of Soldiers but

and elegant speech of one hour and an half endeavoured to convince the audience & the Committee of the absurdity of opposing the extravagant demands of Great Brittain, while we were professing a perfect allegiance to her Authority and supporting her courts of Justice—The Character of the speaker, his great Influence among the People, his known attachment to the liberties of the People, and the artful manner in which he represented the whole subject, as worthy their attention, had an effect, on the assembly that astonished me—

There appeared a general approbation of the measure, and I strongly suspected an universal acquiescence of both Committee & Audience in approving the Doctor's Scheme—I never felt myself in a more mortifying Situation—The anonymous publication—The Meeting of the Trustees of the College but the Day before made up wholly of Presbyterians,—Their President leaving them to attend the meeting & avowing himself the Author of it—The Doctor known to be at the head of the Presbyterian Interest, and Mr. Smith & Myself both Presbyterians, arriving at New Brunswick in the morning, as if intending to go forward & then staying and attending the meeting, altogether looked so like a preconcerted Scheme, to accomplish the End, that I was at my wit's end, to know how to extricate myself from so disagreeable a situation, especially as the measure was totally ag's my Judgment.

On a minutes Conversation with Mr. Smith, I

determined at all events to step forward & leave
my Testimony of the Scheme in toto—Two of the
Committee had delayed the Question by speaking
in favour of it, but no one had spoken in opposition, till I rose, and in a speech of about half an
hour or better, stated my peculiar Situation and endeavoured to show the fallacy of the Doctors Argument,—That his plan was neither founded in Wisdom, Prudence, nor Economy,—That we had chosen
a Continental Congress, to whom we had resigned
the Consideration of our public affairs—That they,
coming from every part of the Union, would best
represent all the Colonies now thus united.—They
would know the true Situation of our Country with
regard to finances, Union & the prospects we had
of a happy reconciliation with the Mother Country—
They would also be possessed of our relative Circumstances with regard to the other Nations of
Europe—In short that they were the only proper
Judges of the measures to be pursued, and that
we had no right to involve them in distress and
trouble by plunging ourselves into measures of so
delicate a nature, until they should advise us in
what manner to proceed etc etc

This opposition wholly unexpected by the Doctor with the great attention of all present, a little
disconcerted him.—but he soon recovered himself,
and began a reply when two or three Gent' of the
Audience came to me & desired that I would inform
the Doctor, that if he proceeded any farther, they

would not be answerable for his safety—I answered, that the request was an unreasonable one.—That I had been the only person present who had opposed him, that he had a right to be heard in reply, and if they disliked the proposition, they ought openly to come forward & to give their opinion—

The Doctor had not spoken twenty minutes, when I observed some person whispering to him— He directly stopped—informed the Chairman, that he found that he was giving offence, and therefor he should say no more on the subject, but hoped that the Committees would return to their respective Counties & consult their Constituents, without coming to any determination on the Subject—

To this I objected, urging the impropriety of breaking up without a Vote, as in that Case the opinion of the meeting would be variously reported in the different Counties, according to each mans political Creed; and the people would by these means be led astray.

The Doctor was a good deal out of humor & contended warmly against a vote—but a large Majority of the Meeting insisted on a Vote, which, being taken, out of 36 Members, there were but 3 or 4 who Voted for the Doctors proposition, the rest rejecting it with great warmth.   Thus ended this first attempt to try the pulse of the People of New Jersey on the Subject of Independence; and yet when advised by the Continental Congress, no part of the Union were more trusty than the State of New Jersey.

Visits the Continental Prisoners in New York to Examine into their Grievances.

In the spring of 1777 General Washington wrote me a letter requesting me to accept of a Commission as Commissary General of Prisoners in the Army of America—I waited on him and politely declined the task urging the wants of the Prisoners & having nothing to supply them—He very kindly objected to the conduct of Gentlemen of the Country refusing to join him in his Arduous struggle,—That he had nothing in View but the Salvation of his Country, but it was impossible for him to accomplish it alone, That if Men of Character & Influence would not come forward & join him in his Exertions all would be lost—Affected by this address, and supposing that I could be of some service to the Prisoners, and at the same time have an Eye on the Military Power & prevent its Incroachment, on the Civil Authority, I consented to accept the Commission on the Generals assurance that I would be supplied by the secret Committee of Congress with hard Money for the relief of Prisoners, and that I should only be subject to his order in the Conduct of my department—

Soon after I had entered on my department, the applications of the Prisoners were so numerous and their distress so urgent, that I exerted every nerve

to obtain Supplies but invain—Excepting £600—
I had rec'd from the Secret Committee in Bills of
Exchange, at my first entrance into the Office—I
could not by any means get a farthing more, except
in Continental Money, which was of no avail in
New York.—I applied to the General describing
my delicate Situation and the continual application
of the Officers, painting their extreme distress, and
urging the assurance they had rec'd that on my
appointment, I was to be furnished with adequate
means for their full relief—The General appeared
greatly distressed & assured me that it was out of
his power to afford me any supplies—I proposed
drawing Clothing from the public Stores, but to
this he objected as not having any thing like a suf-
ficient supply for the Army. He urged my considering & adopting the best means in my power
to satisfy the necessities of the Prisoners, & he
would confirm them—I told him I knew of no
means in my Power but to take what Monies I had
of my own, & to borrow from my friends in New
York, to accomplish the desirable purpose—He
greatly encouraged me to the attempt, promising
me that if I finally met with any loss, he would
divide it with me—On this I began to afford them
some supplies of Provisions over and above what
the Enemy afforded them, which was very small &
very indifferent.

The Complaints of the very cruel treatment our
Prisoners met with, in the Enemy's lines rose to

such a Heighth that in the Fall of this Year, 1777, the General wrote to General Howe or Clinton respecting there complaints & proposing to send an Officer into New York to examine into the truth of them—This was agreed to, and a regular Passport returned accordingly—The General ordered me on this Service—I accordingly went over on the third of Feb 1778 in my own Sloop—supposing that my treatment would be very harsh, I prepared to meet with it in a proper manner. at Staten Island, the Commanding General, put on Board of us a Sergeant & file of Men we arrived at the wharf at New York, a little before Sun down, when I sent the Sergeant to the Commandant of the City (who was General Robertson, who I had formerly known) to inform him of my arrival & request to land. In a very short time, the Sergeant returned, with an answer that I must send to the General my rank & Business before I could be permitted to land—knowing that the General knew both, I was chagrined at this Answer, and immediately turning to the Captain of my Sloop in the presence of the Sergeant, asked him if the Wind would suit to return over the Bay, to which he answered in the affirmative—I then took out my Watch & addressing the Sergeant, told him to return to his General & inform him that I would neither send him my rank or business, as he well knew both, and that if I was not suffered to land in Ten minutes, I should return from whence I came—The Sergeant surprised at such a message to the Commanding General, ran with great haste to deliver this answer, and much sooner than I could have expected, Major Courtland returned with the Sergeant & very politely desired me to land, as he was ordered to conduct me to the Commissary of Prisoners—When I came to Mr. Commissary Lorings, he behaved very civilly, and after taking Tea with him, desired me to attend him to the General.

I found no ceremony of blinding me or any other restraint which I had expected I wore a uniform & sword by my side. The General rec'd me with great politeness and appeared as friendly & sociable as he had used to do before the War—He conversed very freely with me for near two hours, without mentioning anything relative to the manner of my conducting myself while in the Garrison—At length he informed me that lodgings were prepared for me, and the Commissary would wait upon me to them—I answered that my being in a garrisoned Town, was an entire new thing to me, and therefor if I asked anything improper, I hoped it would be imputed to my want of knowledge of military caution—That I had a Brother in Law in the City who was my agent, and therefor should be glad, if consistent with order, to lodge with him—The General, with great politeness assured me that the lodgings were prepared, yet I might go where I pleased, on Condi-

tion of my breakfasting with him in the Morning—
This I promised to do, & retired—Taking it for
granted that I was to be put under the expected
restriction in the Morning, I waited on the General
at Breakfast. he behaved as before with the
greatest civility & good humor—After breakfast
he asked a great many questions about the News
in our lines, and conversed on common Topicks,
but said nothing about my Conduct while in the
City, on which I at last introduced the business on
which I had come.—That I was a stranger to military rule—I knew that I was in a garrisoned
Town, and therefor wished to know what line of
Conduct it was expected that I should pursue—
The General answered me that he knew we had
heard strange stories within our lines of their
Conduct to our Prisoners, that he rejoiced that
General Washington had taken the measure of
sending me in to examine for ourselves, for that
he was sure that we should find them a parcel of
damned lies—that he had ordered every Place I
should choose to visit to be freely opened to me,
and that as I was a gentleman, all that he expected was that I should behave as such, and that
I might use my own pleasure & go where I
pleased—I confess I was surprised at this generous conduct, and immediately replied, that I could
not accept the Gentlemanly offer—That I had come
on a fair and open Business That I had no secrets
to communicate & would not receive any from

any person whatever,—That I could not put myself
so far in their power, as after my departure to
render it possible for them to Charge me with
improper behaviour unworthy my Character, by
communicating or recieving secret intelligence to
or from our Officers—That my intentions were not
only to be convinced myself of the truth of the
treatment the Prisoners had received, but if it had
been cruel, that the General also should be convinced of the fact also, as necessary towards their
relief, That therefor I should not see a Prisoner
or have any communication with one but in the
presence of a british Officer, who I hoped he
would oblige me by appointing to attend me—The
General expressed himself well pleased with the
proposal, and appointed one accordingly, observing
again, that he was sure I should find the reports
we had heard totally false—Accordingly I went
to the Provost, with the Officer, where we found
near 30 Officers from Colonels downwards, in close
confinement in the Gaol in New York. After some
conversation with late Ethan Allen, I told him my
errand, on which he was very free in his abuse of
the British on account of the cruel Treatment he
had rec'd during —— Months close confinement.
We then proceeded up stairs to the Room of their
Confinement. I had the Officers drawn up in a
Ring, and informed them of my mission,—that I
was determined to hear nothing in secret, That I
therefore hoped they would each of them in their

turn report to me faithfully & candidly the Treatment they severeally had recieved—that my design was to obtain them the proper redress, but if they Kept back anything from an improper fear of their keepers, they would have themselves only to blame for their want of immediate redress—That for the purpose of their deliverance the British Officer attended that the British General, should be also well informed of Facts.—On this after some little hesitation from a dread of their keeper, the Provost Martial, One of them began & informed us that they had been confined on the most frivolous pretenses, some for having been oppressors of the friends of Government,—for taking refugees' Property, while officers under command & in obedience to orders—for being out of their bounds of Parole, the week after their return—some confined in the Dungeon for a Night to wait the Censure of General to examine them, & forgot for months—for being Committee Men, &c., &c.—That they had rec'd the most cruel Treatment from the Provost Martial, being locked up in the Dungeon on the most trifling pretenses, such as asking for more water for drink on a hot day than usual—for sitting up a little longer in the Evening than orders allowed—for writing a letter to the General making their Complaints of ill usage & throwing out of the Windows.—That some of them were kept 10, 12 & 14 weeks in the Dungeon on these trifling Pretenses — a Captain Vandyke

had been confined 18 months for being concerned
in setting fire to the City When, on my calling
for the Provost Books, it appeared that he had
been made Prisoner, & closely confined, in the
Provost 4 days before the fire happened—A
Major Paine had been confined 11 months for
killing a Capt. Campbell in the Engagement when
he was taken Prisoner, when, on Examinaation it
appeared that the Captain had been killed in another
part of the Action—The charge was that Major
Paine when taken had no Commission tho' acknowledged by us as a Major—Capt. —— was confined for breaking a soldiers thigh with the but of
his Gun after he was shot down, when the British
Surgeon on examination acknowledged that the
thigh was broken by a Ball, &c., &c., &c. Most of
the cases examined into turned out wholly false or
too trifling to be regarded—It also appeared by
the Declaration of some of the Gent' that their
water would be sometimes, as the Caprice of the
Provost Martial led him, brought up to them in the
Tubs they used in their Rooms, & when the weather
was so hot that they must drink or perish—On
hearing a number of these instances of Cruelty—I
asked who was the Author of them, they answered
the provost keeper—I desired the Officer to call him
up that we might have him face to face—He accordingly came in, and on being informed of what
had passed, he was asked if the Complaints were
true. He, with great Insolence answered, that every

word was true—on which the British Officer, abusing him very much, asked him how he dared to treat Gent' in that cruel Manner, he, insolently putting his hands to his side swore that he was as absolute there as Gen'l Howe was at the head of his Army— I observed to the Officer that now there could be no dispute about Facts as the fellow had acknowledged every word to be true—I stated all the facts in substance & waited again on Gen'l Robertson, who hoped I was quite satisfied of the falsity of the reports I had heard—I then stated to him the facts, and assured him that they turned out worse than any thing we had heard. On his hesitating as to the truth of this assertion, I observed to him the propriety of having an Officer with me, to whom I now appealed for the truth of the facts. He being present confirmed them,—on which the Gen'l expressed great disatisfaction, & promised that the Author of them should be punished. I insisted that the Officers should be discharged from his Power on Parole on long Island as other Officers were—To this after recieving from me a copy of the facts I had taken down, he assented and all were discharged except Seven, who were detained some time before I could obtain their reliese—I forgot to mention that one Officer, Lieut —— was taken Prisoner and brought in with a wound thro' his leg. He was sent to the Provost to be examined the next morning—He was put into the Dungeon & remained there 10 weeks totally forgotten by the

General, and never had his wound dressed except
as he washed it with a little Rum and Water,
given to him by the Centinels thro' the —— hole
out of their own rations. Cap —— & a Cap Chatham were confined with them and their allowance
was 4 lb hard spoiled Biscuit & 2 lb Pork per
week; which they were obliged to Eat raw—while
they were thus confined, for the slightest Complaints, the Provost Martial would come down and
beat them unmercifully with a Rattan & Knock
them down with his fist—After this I visited two
Hospitals of our Sick Prisoners and the Sugar
House; in the two first were 211 Prisoners & in
the last about 190—They acknowledge that for
about two months past they fared pretty well.
being allowed 2 lb of good Beef and a proportion
of flour or Bread per week by Mr Lewis my
Agent over and above the Allowance rec' from the
British which was professed to be $\frac{2}{3}$r Allowance—
but before they had suffered much from the small
allowance they had rec' & that their Bread was
very bad being musty biscuit, but that the British
Soldiers made the same Complaint as to the bread.
—From every account I recieved, I found that
their treatment had been greatly changed for the
better., within a few months past., except at the
Provost. They all agreed that previous to the
capture of Genl Burgoyne, and for some time after,
Their treatment had been cruel beyond measure,
That the prisoners in the French Church, amounting

on an average to 3 & 400, could not all lay down at
once, that from the 15th Oct. to the 1st Jany. they
never recd a single stick of wood, and that for the
most part they eat their Pork Raw, when the Pews
& Door & Wood on Facings failed them for fuel.

But as to my own personal knowledge, I found
Genl Robertson very ready to agree to every measure for alleviating the miseries of War : and very
candidly acknowledged many faults committed by
the inferior Officers, and even the mistakes of the
General himself, by hearkening to the representa-
tions of those around him, He showed me a letter
from Genl Howe who was in Philadelphia. giving
orders that we should not be at liberty to purchase
Blankets within their lines,—and containing a copy
of an Order, I had issued, that they should not
purchase provisions within ours, by way of retaliation but he represented it as if my order was first
—I stated the facts to Genl Robertson who assured
me that Genl Howe had been imposed upon & requested me to state the facts by way of letter
which he immediately wrote to Genl Howe. urging
the propriety of reversing his orders, which afterwards he did in a very hypocritical manner as will
appear hereafter.

One Day Calling on Genl Robertson he asked
me if I had any objection against a free private
political Conversation. I answered that I could
not have any.—He asked me up into his Bed
Room, and began by asking me, why so much

blood was shed, among those who were once breth-
ern, when it was apparent that no valuable end
could be answered by it. Why no one had yet
stepped forth to stop so unnatural a breach & prevent the cutting each other's throats—I replied,
that no good reason could in my opinion be assigned—That the fault lay with them—They had invaded our Land—we had not troubled them—that
all we had asked was to be heard—That this was
refused and War and desolation was brought by
them into our Country.

It was therefor with them to make propositions,
that we might know which it was they would be
at. That we were not only strangers to & ignorant
in the Art of War and almost wholly unprepared
for it, but were lovers of Peace & only wished to
enjoy our Habitations in quietness, without quar-
relling with any one.—— He expressed himself
very strongly agt the war, as an unnatural destruction of each other by which nothing valuable was
to be obtained,—That he was authorized to assure
me that if any one would step forward & heal the
unhappy difference, that he should be rewarded in
any manner he should ask, even to a Pension of
Ten Thousand Pounds Sterling—I observed to him
that there could be no necessity for this, that the
Americans were desirous of Peace, and would
eagerly seize every opportunity of embracing it,
but the proposition from the nature of the thing
must come from them.

He observed that Lord Howe & Genl Howe had been authorized to make peace with us on almost any Terms. I assured him that I had been conversant with the proceedings of Congress & the knowledge of Genl Washington and I did not believe that any such thing was known. After a little reflection, he insisted that the fact was so, and that Lord Howe had actually written an account of it to Genl Washington before his landing, while off the Hook at Sea.—On my repeating my disbelief of it, he told me that this was one of the evils of the present dispute.—That a parcel of Demagogues had professed themselves of the Govt and kept the people in entire Ignorance of the true principles of the differences between us, That he was sure if the people of America were left to themselves, They had too much good sense to continue the Breach, after such offers of Peace on our own Terms—at last starting as from a reverie, he said we must know it, as he had seen lord Howe's letter in our News Papers, I asked him if he did not know that Lord Howe's Authority went no farther than merely to grant Pardons, &c. He seemed confused and said that any Agreement he made would be ratified by the Parliament of Great Brittain—I then reminded him that the war had been brought on by the British Ministry having refused to suffer Parliament only to hear us, that being the sum of our last Petition and whether (as he had said, he knew many very

sensible and Worthy men in America) he thought
those sensible men would ever submit to make a
Treaty with any British Commissioners (and
thereby loose the Friendship of France), and
Trust to a British Ministry (whose treatment had
hitherto been so unworthy Men of Probity or Political understanding) to have ratified by Parliament.   He now seemed a little chagrined, and said
with some seeming petulance, that he did not
know what the American Gentn. had done with
their Oaths of Allegiance—Indeed Sir, I know
not how you have got over, your Oath of Allegiance for I know you have taken one. I answered
that it had been matter of some difficulty to me
till I was legally discharged by an Act of the
British Parliament.   He said he had never heard
of any such Act.   I told him (much in the language he had used in the beginning to me) that I
had long known the misfortune of the British
Officers.   That they were kept hoodwinked and
in total ignorance of the Causes and Reasons
of the War in which they were engaged—That
they were obliged to obey & fight in every cause
whether right or wrong.—That I supposed that
this Act was kept from getting to their knowledge, but I knew the fact, and had seen it in St
Jame's Chronicle published by Authority.   He
assured me that it must be a congressional false-
hood and that no such Act, had ever been passed.
I then asked him if he was acquainted with the

British Constitution—He answered in the affirmative. I asked him what he thought of Allegiance & Protection. He said they always went together, and that without Protection no Allegiance was due. I replied Have you never seen Sir, an act of Parliament putting all the Colonies (friends & foes) out of the King's protection—The Old Gentn. seemed alarmed at his Confession, and with warmth said.—A damned act.—a damned Act—I told the Ministry so at the time—They were distracted.— A damned Act.—let us go down Stairs—and our Conversation Ended—

MEETS THE BRITISH COMMISSIONER AT GERMANTOWN, TO EXCHANGE THE HESSIAN PRISONERS, AND THE CONVERSATION THAT TOOK PLACE THEREAT.

In the Spring of 1778 about the month of May or beginning of June, I was appointed by Genl. Washington to meet a Commissioner on the part of the British, at Germantown to Exchange the Hessian Prisoners in our Custody—On my arrival I found the British Commissioner was the same General Robertson, who had brought out a Gentn. with him, who had been an acquaintance of mine, a very sensible, prudent, Genteel Man—After doing our Business and dining together—This Gentn

asked me if I would walk in the Garden with him
I readily agreed. when there he asked me if I
had any objection to a confidential Political Conversation—I said I could have none.—He told me
that the British exceedingly regretted our unhappy
dispute—That they were convinced, it could end in
no substantial good to either party—That they
were now convinced of the propriety of healing
the breach.—That if any person would undertake
to settle the unhappy dispute, he was authorized
to promise them anything from a Dukedom to Ten
Thousand Sterling pr annum. To this I replied
as before to Genl Robertson, that offers of that
kind could have no effect on men who were acting
from Principle, That America wanted Peace &
Quietness.—That the British had invaded us, and
it was on her part to say what she wanted.—He
said he came authorized in the fullest manner, to
offer a Carte Blanche, it should be signed by
proper Authority and I might fill it up myself.—
I told him that I was too well acquainted with the
British Govt. & of the nature of the dispute, not
to know that such an offer was merely delusion &
that it could only tend to decieve, for they never
designed nor could do any such thing—He in the
most positive Terms assured me that it was all real
and nothing could give more pleasure to the Govt.
than to have it agreed to—I answered that I did
not doubt his honesty in the business but well
knew that he was imposed upon.—He however

fields in despair. In his walk he met with a Citizen who lived in the suburbs, with whom he fell into Conversation & fully told him his distress, as a Merchant whose remittance had failed, and who in consequence knew not where to get a meal of Victuals. This man generously took him to his house and agreed to board him till he should get returns from his friends—After waiting sometime longer and finding no hope of seeing Count De Vergennes, he determined on returning to America Re Infecta.—He had actually packed up his little Wardrobe and was preparing to embark, When in the Afternoon he rec' Letters announcing The Declaration of Independence by Congress and the Action of General Arnold on Lake Champlain with the British fleet, within two hours after : he recd a Card from Count De Vergennes requesting his company immediately on business of importance Mr Deane being exceedingly chagrined with the treatment he had recd refused to go.—The next morning just as he had got up from Bed, the Sieur Gerard called upon him from the Count De Vergennes insisting on his calling & Breakfasting with him.—He again refused, but on Mr Gerard's pressing it with warmth, he agreed to go—when he arrived at the Counts he was received as an old acquaintance & treated with as much familiarity & friendship as if there had been a long acquaintance between them——a long Conversation took place, on the American Contest when Mr Deane acquainted him with his mission and his wants, The Count made the most positive declaration ags doing any thing to promote the disaffection of her Colonies with Great Britain,—That France should support her faith with her good ally Great Brittain, and could not hearken to any proposition inconsistent with her Treaty with that Power, and so they parted, with some assurances however that his personal wants should be supplied.

The next morning a Man under the name Monsr Beaumarchais whom Mr Deane considered as sent by Count De Vergennes called upon him and told him that he had heard that he (Mr Deane) was a Bermudian Merchant and that he was desirous of Contracting with some person for a quantity of Merchandise—That he (Beaumarchais) had been a Courtier & had been banished on some affront given at Court—that lately he had permission to return, That he was just entering into Mercantile Speculations & if they could agree, he should be glad to serve him. Mr Deane took the hint, told him that he wanted Warlike Stores, from a flint to a Thirty Six pounds Great Gun.—That he could only purchase on a long Credit, to be paid on Instalments, and that he must also be supplied with a Vessel or Vessels to carry them to America. Beaumarchaise answered that it would take a long time to manufacture so large a demand, Deane said they must be provided immediately as his wants admitted of no delay.—He replied that he was

acquainted with the KING'S ARMORER and perhaps
he might be persuaded upon to lend him what was
wanted, and he would restore them as they were
manufactured,—In fine an old frigate was immediately loaded with every thing that was wanted,—
But Just before she was ready to sail the British
Minister found it out; and made a spirited memorial to the King A Violent Proclamation was the
Consequence, threatening death and destruction to
all concerned in so wicked an Attempt, and ordering
the frigate to be immediately unloaded, she was
accordingly unloaded in the day. and the Loading
put on Board of three more merchantmen at Night,
and they sailed in a few days, two of them arriving
safe in America, to the great relief of the American
Army.—All this was a profound secret, but was
well understood by Congress to be a present from
the King of France, but could not be contained on
their Journals. After this the famous Thos. Paine
being the Secretary to the Secret Committee and
under oath of Secrecy, or some writer in the Public
Papers, divulged the whole business in one of his
publications—This brought the French Minister
forward by a warm memorial to Congress, Who
found themselves obliged to deny the King of
France having any thing to do with the Transaction
declaring it to be a common Mercantile Contract
with Beaumarchais. He in his turn have since
taken advantage of this acknowledgment; and have
called on Congress to pay the whole purchase
money with interest—

THE STORY OF JOHN AITKEN, *alias* "JOHN THE PAINTER," WHO DESTROYED THE BRITISH NAVAL STORES AT PORTSMOUTH, ENGLAND.

Mr Deane also related to me the following Story

That while he was in Paris, a stranger, rather advanced in Years, called upon him and requested to talk with him in Private, where no one could know what they were about, Deane surprised at such a request, was rather on his guard, and interrogated the Stranger as to his business, but he could get nothing from him, till they should go into a private Room. Deane suspected him, as an emisary from the British Ministry, but at length, determined to gratify him. When alone he made many excuses for his errand, but finally told him that he was an American Citizen, tho a Scotch man by birth, that he had lived in Amboy in New Jersey, where he had a comfortable House.—That while the British Army was in possession of Amboy, they had suspected his principles, and treated him very ill in various ways, and finally burnt down his house, and gave him much personal insult. That he had determined on revenge and had at last determined on killing King George, for which purpose he had come to Europe. That he had been to England & laid his plan, and was now ready to execute it, but thought it his duty to make Mr

Deane acquainted with it, as the Minister from his Country & to take his advice,—that he passed by the name of John the Painter.—Mr Deane was much surprised at this communication and at first thot him deranged. He then suspected that he might have been sent as a sham by the British Minister—After talking with him a little & finding him determined, he desired him to call again.

The next day he returned discovering as determined a resolution as ever. Mr Deane reasoned with him, that it was mean & cowardly to attempt to assassinate a Man in cold Blood, when he had never injured him personally, he answered that his servants had insulted, abused & finally ruined him and he would have revenge, and that no earthly Consideration should prevent him. He developed his whole plan, and Mr D—— said he was surprised at the wisdom of it. to accomplish the End, as he seemed to have laid it in such a manner as to render success certain. Mr D. told him that if he must have revenge he should take it in a manly, generous way. He should go into the American Army, and meet his Enemy fairly in the field, That if he could meet King George at the head of his Army in the field. and should kill him in a fair battle, no one could object, or if he could succeed in killing his Generals or Army, in open Contest, it would be lawful, but the private assassination of an innocent man, off his Guard & suspecting no ill, would be abhored by all mankind. that he could not encourage him or give him aid in so wicked a purpose but must do every thing to dissuade him from it & to prevent it if possible.—on this he left him.— When he returned again, he came in a little frantick, saying, I thank you sir, I thank you sir. I confess it is unlawful to lift my hand agt the Lords anointed. You have convinced me. I will not lift my hand agt the Lords Anointed. But I am determined to have the Naval Stores at Portsmouth, Deane answered, that as that would tend to weaken the Enemy in carrying on the War, if he could accomplish it, he could have no objection, but would aid him in it. He said he could do it, & would go over to England & reconoitre the Place. Deane reminded him, that if he was Catched he would assurdly loose his life. He said he should not attempt to save it. He was an old man. He had no connections, and whether he died now or three or four years hence it was a matter of but little consequence to him, so that he could but get revenge. He accordingly went to Portsmouth & on his return, communicated to Mr Deane his whole Plan, with the instrument made of Tin & nearly finished with which he was to accomplish it. The Scheme was well laid & promised success. Some days after he came again, and said now I know you will think me a rascal. I am come to borrow Money. I have expended all I have. I want one Guinea to carry me to Portsmouth. Deane told him if that was all he should

have it, he gave it to him and he went of.—Deane
received the following acct. of his proceedings from
a friend who attended his examination before the
Privy Council—That he arrived at Portsmouth &
took up lodgings at a very poor Womans, at the
skirts of the town.—Early next morning he went
out to reconoitre. The old woman anxious to
know who or what her guest was, had the curi-
osity to look into his bundle. She found a shirt &
pair of stockings with a Tin Machine, which she
could not comprehend—John the Painter wanted
a Top to his machine & took it to a Tinman & had
one made.—In the Evening he accomplished his
purpose & Consumed near £100,000 sterl. worth
of Stores. In the Morning every Person in the
Town were ordered to report if any stranger had
lodged there.—The old woman reported John the
Painter, with the extraordinary tin Machine. The
Tinman reported his making a Top for it—John
was fixed upon as the Incendiary, and taking for
granted that he was sent properly prepared for the
purpose, and that relays of Horse were prepared
for his Escape, Horsemen were sent on every
Road, with orders to pursue and take up any &
every person they found riding Post. — By day
light in the Morning John had taken his Bundle &
truged on foot up to London.—about noon the
Horsemen sent on that Road came up with John,
and asked him if he had seen any person on Horse-
back riding Post that day. John answered in the

Negative & requested to know the reason for their Enquiry—They related the Story of the Fire, and that they were in search for the Incendiary.   John told them they were wholly mistaken in their pursuit for that he was the Man who had set fire to the stores, and gave them his reasons for doing it. at first they thought him crazy, but on his repeating it with some particular circumstances.—they siezed him & brought him back to Portsmouth— He was then recognized by the old Woman & Tinman, and sent to London where he was examined before the Privy Council, He candidly told them the whole Story, declaring that he should certainly have killed the King had not Mr Deane dissuaded him from it & convinced him that it was unlawful to lift his hand agt the Lords anointed— That he was ready to die & he did not care how soon.   He denied having any accomplice, and that he rejoyced in having obtained revenge for the cruelties with which he had been treated by the British Army.   He was tryed condemned & hanged—a very unfair & false acct. of his Examination was published & no Notice taken of Mr Deane's having saved the Kings Life.

For English statement see Gentleman's Magazine for 1777.

An Account of the Frenchman who Poisoned American Prisoners, in New York, and was Rewarded, for so doing, by General Howe.

When the British Army took possession of New York, they found a Frenchman in Goal, under Condemnation for Burglery & Robbery. He was liberated. He was a very loos, ignorant Man. Had been a Servant. This fellow was set over our Prisoners in the Hospital, as a Surgeon, tho' he knew not the least principle of the Art. Dr McHenry, a Physician of Note in the American Army, and then a Prisoner, finding the extreme ignorance of this man, and that he was really murdering our people, remonstrated to the British Director of the Hospital, & refused visiting our sick Prisoners if this Man was not dismissed. A British Officer convinced that he had killed several of our People, lodged a complaint agt him when he was ordered to be tryed by a Court Martial, but the Morning before the Court were to set, this Officer was ordered off to St Johns, and the Criminal was discharged, for want of Evidence. During this man having the Charge of our Prisoners in the Hospital two of our Men deserted from the Hospital & came into our Army when they were ordered to me for Examination. They

Joined in this story. That they were sick in the Hospital under the care of the above Frenchman— That he came & examined them, and gave to each of them a dose of Physick to be taken immediately—a Young Woman their Nurse made them some private signs not to take the Physick immediately—After the Doctor was gone, she told them that she suspected the Physick was poison— That she had several times heard this Frenchman say that he would have Ten Rebels dead in such a room and five dead in such a Room, the next morning, and it always so happened. They asked her what they should do—she told them their only chance was to get off sick as they were, that she would help them out, and they must shift for themselves. — They accordingly got off safe & brought the Physick with them.—This was given to a Surgeons Mate who afterwards reported, that he gave it to a Dog, and that he died in a very short time.—I afterwards saw an acct in the London Paper of this same Frenchman being taken up in England for some Crime and condemned to dye.—At his Execution he acknowledged the fact of his having murdered a great number of Rebels in the Hospital at New York, by poyson.—That on his reporting to Genl Howe the number of the Prisoners dead, he raised his pay—He further confessed that he poisoned the wells used by the American flying Camp, which caused such an uncommon Mortality among them in the year 1776.

CAPTURE OF YORKTOWN.—COUNT DE GRASSE
THREATENS TO WITHDRAW THE FRENCH
TROOPS—WASHINGTON'S EXPEDIENT WHICH
LED TO THE CAPITULATION.

At the Siege of York Town ; the French Troops
brought out by Count De Grasse, were absolutely
necessary to compleat the line of Circumvallation,
and perfect the siege—about 2 days before the
Capture. The Count sent word to Genl Washington that he should within 48 Hours withdraw
those Troops & that he must provide accordingly
—This was in effect raising the Siege. Genl Washington remonstrated agt it in vain. He sent the
Marquiss La Fayette on Board the Fleet to dissuade Count de Grasse from so ruinous a measure.
he obstinately presisted, and said his orders were
positive & not discretionary.

Genl Washington finding that nothing but
storming the enemies lines would prevent the raising of the Siege, and that would unnecessarily
occasion the loss of great numbers on both sides,
to avoid which he fell on the following expedient—
He sent out Col Hamilton with some other officers
with a Flag of Truce on some business—They
were met half way by a number of British officers,
They carried with them something to eat and drink
In Conversation they mentioned to the British Officers. their concern for them as Gentn. & Soldiers

that the American Army had determined to Storm
their lines.—that the American Soldiery & Country
People were so exasperated at the Conduct of the
British to the Southward, that they could not answer
for the Consequences. as they did not think they
could be restrained by authority and Discipline—
That they knew Genl Washington's humane Tem-
per, and his wish to avoid the unnecessary shedding
of blood. That in Case of a Capitulation the same
Terms the British gave to our Troops at Charles
Town, with the addition of the Officers wearing
side Arms & being immediately sent on their parole
into New York they believed might be obtained.
That they did not wish their names to be mentioned
&c &c   Within a few Hours after their return pro-
posals for surrendering on Terms were sent out, and
the capitulation took place—Count De Grasse remained several days (notwithstanding the Positive
Nature of his Orders) to enjoy the pleasure of the
surrender, the rejoicings &c &c.   Genl Washington
then earnestly requested his landing a Body of
American Troops near Eden Town North Carolina, that the British in that neighborhood might
be surprised, but he obstinately refused, Then he
spent twice the time necessary for the purpose doing
nothing before he left the Coast.

When the messenger brought the News of this
Capitulation to Congress, it was necessary to furnish him with hard money for his expenses, There
was not a sufficiency in the Treasury to do it, and

the Members of Congress, of which I was one, each paid a Dollar to accomplish it.—

Before the Capture & at the first preparation for the Siege, before Count De Grasse arrived, Genl Clinton sent a row Boat well manned with a Confidential Officer along the Coast to get into York Town with a letter to Lord Cornwallis, setting forth his situation and the impossibility of his relieving him with a fleet till a certain day, and encouraging him to hold out till that period—The Boat was driven on shore some where near Egg Harbor and the Crew taken and brought to Philadelphia One of the men discovered in private, where they were bound & that the confidential letter had been hidden under a certain large Stone on the Shore by the Officer— A Person was sent to the Place & brought it to Congress. It was in Cypher and after some trouble it was discovered to be in three different Cyphers, However it was decyphered by a Mr Lovel a Member of Congress from Boston, after about two days labour.—The original letter was carefully returned to the Stone or some means used so that it finally got to Lord Cornwallis, but not before Count De Grasse's arrival, and having the Copy fairly translated—By this means he was enabled to counteract all their intended Meneuvres.—

The Siege of York Town was merely acsidental —General Washington the Fall and Winter before, had planned with a Committee of Congress, the storming of the works at New York and the

repossession of that City—He communicated his
design to the French General and the arrival of
Count De Grasse with a French fleet was part of
the Plan—Requisitions on the different States for
a supply of Men. to the necessary amount; was
duly made by Congress, They to be in the field
by a given day.

The necessary preparation, especially a number
of very large battering Cannon were provided, a
little before the expected reinforcement. The
Marquiss La Fayette was very hard pressed by the
British in Virginia—he had not Men enough to
make head agt them, and was driven to a depend-
ance on Manouevering altogether—He wrote to
Genl Washington for aid alleging the impossibility
of maintaining his ground without a reinforcement,
General Washington answered him by letting him
into his Designs on New York.—That he must do
as well as he could with the force he had, as he
could not spare him a man.—but when the enemy
should discover his intention it would work a diver-
sion in the Marquiss' favour. This letter we sent by
the mail. This was captured in passing thro' Jersey and the letter fell into the Enemys Hands.
Thus his whole design was destroyed, with the
weakness of the Marquiss.—However preparation
went on, but the Day for the assembling the
Troops arrived, and the supplies did not more than
fill up the places of the sick & Dead thro' the
Winter—The General remonstrated to Congress of

the State in vein.—His numbers were not half suf-
ficient to justify an attack on New York. He
feared he should become the dirision of the French
Army & the Enemy—His mind ever full of re-
sources, immediately suggested the plan of taking
advantage of the Enemies knowledge of his plans.
—He wrote to congress, had a confidential & secret
Committee appointed (of which I was one) immediately assembled the Army, (such as it was) in
the County of Essex & Morris, near New York.
Had the large battering Cannon sent on at a Heavy
Expense from Philadelphia—Erected very even
at Chatham about Eleven Miles above Elizabeth-
Town—Every one was on Tip toe with the expectation of soon entering into New York,—On the
Morning of his intended departure, about day
light, he sent for an old Inhabitant of New York
who lived in the Neighborhood and who was suspected of giving Intelligence to the Enemy.—and
put a number of important Questions to him,
about the situation of the Country in & about
Middle town & Sandy Hook in the County of
Monmouth where the man was born & bred.—also
as to the state of the land on the opposite shore on
Long Island—with regard to landing of Troops,
Water &c. alleging that he was fond of knowing
the situation of different parts of the Country as in
the course of the war he might unexpectedly be
called into that part of the Country—He urged
upon him the most profound secrecy and by no

means to lisp a word of what had passed between them—In one hour the Army marched apparently for Princeton which might be a good road to Monmouth, if a deception was intended—I happened to be in the neighborhood of the Army, and about Ten O'clock called on the Man on whom the Genl. had enjoined so much secrecy, and to Convince me that the Siege of New York was determined & that by the way of Monmouth & Long Island, he told me every thing that had passed between him & the General, and I doubt not but that the British Genl. had it also the same night. The British unsuspected any other design, till they were informed that the American Army had passed the Delaware.—Then it was too late—When they arrived at Philadelphia, the Army discovered great discontent at not receiving certain arrears of pay, long withheld from them. It was thought neither prudent nor safe to proceed farther without making pay at least, in part. Money was also wanted to hire Vessels & other means to proceed down the Chesapeak Bay. The Treasury was empty. Congress had no means to raise the money.—Requisition had been resorted to in vain.—In this exigency the vigorous exertions of the Honl. Robt Morris the superintendent of Finances, relieved their distress.—He went out among his Mercantile & other Friends, and borrowed on his own responsibility upwards of 30,000 dollars which answered every purpose, and the Army soon appeared before York-Town——

CARTEL FOR EXCHANGE OF PRISONERS.—EX-
PLAINING THE PERFIDY OF GENERAL HOWE
AND THE MANNER IN WHICH THE CONTINENTAL
CONGRESS INSULTED GENERAL WASHINGTON.

In the Winter of 1778 while laying at Valley
Forge, both Armies called loudly for the Exchange
of Prisoners.—Propositions were accordingly made
by the British to which Congress agreed, by giving
full powers to appoint Commissioners to meet a like
number on the part of the British for the Purpose
—The General accordingly appointed Col Hamilton, Col Harrison, Col Grayson, & myself.—Genl
Howe appointed Col O'Harah, Col Stevens & Capt
Fitz-Patrick, and we were to meet at German
Town.—Previous to the meeting, as it was a matter
quite new to us, we proposed a meeting of General
Officers with Genl Washington, that we might dis-
cuss the business before them and know their opin-
ions.—About this Time Congress sent a committee
of their Body, into the Army to reform it Genl
Washington called this committee to the meeting.
—Genl Washington sat as Chairman—We dis-
cussed the matter over.—The Committee of Congress soon discovered their Sentiments agt an
Exchange and urged it as the opinion of Congress.
That settling this Cartel should be merely ostensible
for the purpose of satisfying the Army and throwing the blame on the British, but true policy

required us to avoid an Exchange of Prisoners just at the opening of the Campaign.—We absolutely refused to undertake the Business on these principles, if we went, we were determined to make the best Cartel we could for the liberation of our Prisoners,—That we would not be made Instruments in so dishonorable a measure—Genl Washington also executed it, and said his Troops looked up to him as their protector, and that he would not suffer an opportunity to be lost, of liberating every Soldier who was then in Captivity let the Consequence be what it might, The Committee were much disgusted and soon left the Army, (whom they gave much dissatisfaction) and returned to Congress—Before the meeting of the Commissioners General Washington, recd a resolution of Congress couched in the most insulting Terms, setting forth that he had appointed Commissioners to settle the Cartel, whom he knew held principles adversary to the true interests of America &c &c. On this I applied to the General & desired to be excused from the service.—He refused, ordered us to the Duty, and told us to make the best treaty in our power, and he would ratify it, and take the risque upon himself. In the month of June after this I went as a delegate to Congress, and the first thing I did was to search the secret minutes for this resolution of Congress, determined to have them expunged from the Minutes.—Not being able to find it, I applied to President Lawrence, to know where I might find it,—He laughed & said that Congress was so ashamed of the measure that was run upon them by the Committee from the Army, that in two or three days after, they had expunged the whole from their minutes.—

On the —— day of —— 1778 the Commissioners set out with a Captains Guard of Horse for German Town—where we met the British Commisrs with great Ceremony.—It had been previously agreed that the Town should be neutral Ground. while our Business lasted, and no Troops but our different Guards should enter,—we exchanged our Powers— and agreed to Dine together,—we were very sociable—We had previously obtained the Characters of our opponents and were convinced that they depended much on out drinking us, we knew Coll Grayson was a match for any of them, and therefor left all that part of the business with him.—They soon found themselves foiled—The next day we met, and objected to their Powers not being sufficiently full, and proposed that as they were Military Men, They should take the lead we being wholly unacquainted with the business and that they should propose a plan of a Cartel, which we might be considering, till they renewed their Powers.—They accepted it, and as we had forseen drew out from among their Papers, a Cartel ready drawn up in form.—To this we had nothing to do but object & propose amendments, which they were not prepared to confute, and easily fell into our measures. It soon appeared that neither of them had ever considered the subject, but depended on the Draught prepared for them.

The Third day we were going on very well, and should soon have finished much to our satisfaction, had we not been guilty of a blunder, which ruined us. The British commissioners after Dinner told us, that they had engaged to attend a grand Ball that was given that evening in the City, and earnestly solicited that we would gratify them by consenting to them going into the City, when they would mention their objections to their powers, and they would be out early in the morning, as it was but 7 Miles, we could not well refuse—They accordingly went, and I suppose reported to Genl Howe their progress—The next morning, They came out in good time and we proceed to business.—When we had finished for the morning, Col O'Hara addressing himself to us, said, that however disagreeable the Task was to them, and however contrary to their first Ideas, it was their positive orders from Genl Howe to inform us, that he did not consider German Town Neutral ground, after we adjoined for the night, and a reasonable time allowed for us to return to our army.—That it was only in obedience to positive orders, that they could have been prevailed upon to communicate this to us. We immediately started at the proposition, gathered up the Papers on the Table, and told them, we understood Genl Howe's meaning that we considered ourselves ill used by such a breach of public Faith, and therefore should, after Dinner, return to Head Quarters, and not to meet again.—They pretended to be much hurt with our Idea of its being a breach of the public Faith, and made many Excuses. We persisted in our resolution,—They finding they could make no impression on us, invited themselves to dine with us.—We immediately perceived their drift was to keep us engaged till it was too late to go, or by drinking freely to prevent us.—We were on our guard & set Col. Grayson to manage them They accordingly sat after dinner with Grayson while we were preparing to go off, till they could scarcely sit upright. Just before sundown they were put on their Horses & went for the City. It now became indeed too late for us to go, we therefore determined to set off by daylight in the morning. we breakfasted before it was scarcely light, and just as we were going off, a Trumpet was heard, and a flag appeared. They brought a letter from the Genl. begging we would delay an hour or two, and they would be out with us again,—but we refused and set off for Head Quarters. Genl Washington approved of our proceedings, and wrote a very tart letter to Genl Howe, charging him with a breach of his pledged faith,—He in answer made very poor excuses, saying that he was misunderstood and hoped that matters would be set right by another Meeting at New Town.—After some hesitation on our part and warm solicitation on the part of the british, another meeting was agreed to at New Town about

20 miles from Philadelphia. Genl Howe expressly & unequivocally pledging his Faith for a positive neutrality.——

Here we continued disputing their powers &c proceeding in the business for Ten Days. When the Cartel was just finished, Col O'Harah in walking out with us, addressed us thus, Gentn: you have behaved, since we have been together, with so much propriety and as Gentlemen, that we feel hurt at any kind of Hypocricy or unfair dishonorable Conduct on our part, which our obedience to orders may oblige us to use. We can therefor no longer keep a secret from you which you ought to know, Tho' we trust for our sakes you will keep entirely to yourselves.—We have spent a great deal of Time disputing about the insufficiency of our Powers &c in making a Cartel with you, at the same time knowing that Genl Howe has no authority to agree to it, which is the true cause of our powers appearing as they do. We have it therefore in positive orders from him that when we can prolong the business no longer to make some excuse & to break off the Treaty—This we consider as dishonorable Conduct, and merely done to satisfy the British Army & try to throw the blame on you, but this is our situation and we candidly reveal it to you in Confidence, to free yourselves from blame. It is therefore in vain for us to spend longer time in settling the Treaty.— let us continue together till our stores are exhausted & then seperate. — We acknowledged ourselves greatly surprised at this unofficerlike Conduct in a British General at the head of such an Army.—but we knew the effect of orders & that they must be obeyed—that perhaps we might make such a report to our General as might give them offence, or they might do the same, and displease us. We therefore proposed, that we should in writing make our objections to their Powers as insufficient for the purpose being essentially defective for settling a Cartel. That they should answer it and we would reply.—That their written Papers should be our mutual report.—To this with great difficulty they agreed & not without the aid of Capt Fitzpatrick, who approved of it at once. The Papers were drawn up accordingly, and these formed the bases of our Report, and we seperated.— At the taking leave Col O'Harah said, now if I am ever taken prisoner, I shall call on Col Hamilton,—Col Harrison, Col Boudinot &c and I expect you'll immediately come to my aid & take care of me.—And if any you are taken Prisoners, call upon us & we will return the compliment.—At the capitulation of York Town, Lord Cornwallis being sick, Col O'Harah, the second in command, delivered up his sword on the Parade to Genl Lincoln, and immediately called out for Col Hamilton. He came up.—now sir, said he, perform your promise tho' when you made it, I little thought that I should ever have an opportunity of requiring your performance of it. — Col Hamilton accordingly took care of him.

LYDIA DARRAH CONVEYS THE NEWS OF GENERAL HOWE'S MOVEMENTS TO ELIAS BOUDINOT, WHEN THE BRITISH WERE IN POSSESSION OF PHILADELPHIA.

BRITISH ARMY AT CHESTNUT HILL.

In the Autumn of 1777 the American Army lay some time at White Marsh. I was then Commissary Genl of Prisoners, and managed the Intelligence of the Army.—I was reconoitering along the Lines near the City of Philadelphia.—I dined at a small Post at the rising Sun abt three miles from the City.— After Dinner a little poor looking insignificant Old Woman came in & solicited leave to go into the Country to buy some flour—While we were asking some Questions, she walked up to me and put into my hands a dirty old needlebook, with various small pockets in it. surprised at this, I told her to return, she should have an answer—On Opening the needlebook, I could not find any thing till I got to the last Pocket, Where I found a piece of Paper rolled up into the form of a Pipe Shank.—on un-rolling it I found information that Genl Howe was coming out the next morning with 5000 Men—13 pieces of Cannon—Baggage Waggons, and 11 Boats on Waggon Wheels. On comparing this with other information I found it true, and immedi-ately rode Post to head Quarters—According to

my usual Custom & agreeable to orders rec from
Genl W. I first related to him the naked facts without comment or Opinion—He rec. it with much
thoughtfulness, I then gave him my opinion, that
Genl Howe's design was to Cross the Deleware
under pretense of going for New York.—Then in
the Night to recross the Deleware above Bristol &
come suddenly on Our Rear, when we were totally
unguarded and cut off all our Baggage, if not the
whole Army.—He heard me without a single observation, being deep in thought. I repeated my
observations. He still was silent—supposing myself
unattended to—I earnestly repeated my Opinion,
with urging him to order a few redoubts thrown
up in our rear, as it was growing late.—The Genl
Answered me, Mr Boudinot the Enemy have no business in our rear. The Boats are designed to deceive
us.—To morrow morning by day light you will find
them coming down such a bye Road on our left.
Then calling an Aid du Camp ordered a line thrown
up along our whole front at the foot of the Hill.
As I was quartered on that very Bye Road with 6
or 8 other Officers, a Mile in front of our Army,
and no Pickett advanced of us. This opinion
made a deep Impression upon me Tho' I thot the
General under a manifest mistake.—I returned to
my Quarters first obtaining a Pickett to be put on
that road in Advance. When I got home the
Officers were informed of the News. and my opinion that we should loose our Baggage at least. the

next morning. That our General was at least out in his Judgment, but repeated his last words.—Proposed it as a matter of prudence to have our Horses saddled & the Servs ordered to have them at the door on the first alarm gun being fired—About three O'clock in the Morning we were roused by the Alarm Guns.—We immediately mounted and by Sunrise, The British was in possession of our Quarters down the Bye Road, mentioned by Genl Washington.—I then said that I never would again set up any Judgment agt. his—The Enemy remained several days encamped on Chestnut Hill & Genl Washington opposite to him—On the Evening of the 2d or 3d day. Genl Washington was informed of some very harsh and severe speeches made by a Committee from Congress, of whom Robt Morris was one, relative to Genl Washington for not attacking the British & putting an End to the War at once. and declaring that if he did not do it, further opposition to the British was vain &c &c. The fact was that both parties were as strongly covered, that the assailant in all probability would have been beaten, and the essential interests of America required that the Americans should gain the Battle—However Genl Washington being exceedingly hurt with these Observations & hard speeches. determined at all events to hazard an attack & let the Committee abide the Consequences.

Accordingly he detached Genl Wayne with his Brigade to advance on the Enemy, into the Valley

between the two Armies, & near the foot of Ches-
nut Hill, to be ready in the morning—Another
Brigade was advanced part of the way towards
him.—A spy who was in our Camp immediately
on Wayne's moving, carried the intelligence to the
British General. A skirmish was had in the day
and one of our Militia Generals wounded. & taken
Prisoner—He was put into a Room adjoining one
in which a British Aid du Camp lodged. He over-
heard an Officer come in & tell him that the Rebels
were advancing to make an attack the next morning, and that their retreat was ordered by the British
General.—When the American Troops began their
movement next morning at the dawn of day not a
British soldier was to be seen.—The light Horse
persued & came up & harassed the rear of the
British a few Miles from Philadelphia.—Thus the
defeat of the American Army was again providen-
tially prevented. for we were by no means equal to
the attack as the British were so strongly posted,
and our Army made up of undisciplined Men.

Providential Escape of the American Army, at Morris Town, New Jersey.

Another providential Escape of our Army happened at Morris Town in the year 1777–8—Our Army was exceedingly reduced so that 3000 effective men were the full amount of the whole. & those very poorly found.   To prevent this being known Genl Washington distributed them by 2 & 3 in a House, all along the main Roads round Morris Town for miles, so that the General expectation among the Country people was, that we were 40000 strong.

Genl Howe desirous of knowing our real strength. sent over a Gentn of some character. a Mercht in New York, as a spy into our Camp.—He told sad stories about the treatment he had recd from the British and that he had deserted from them.   The Adjutant Genl. finding from several Circumstances that he was really a Spy. applied to Genl Washington for an order to take him up and confine him.—The Genl examined into the Circumstances & finding the suspicions well supported, forbid the Adjutant General from touching him, but ordered him to go home & immediately to draw returns from every Brigadier in the Army of the number of their Brigade, making the Army to consist of about 12,000 effective Men &c &c to place these in the paper holes on his Desk, and then to get introduced to the Spy., and invite him to lodge with him.—To endeavor to get him to sup with him alone,—About 9 O'clock in the Evening to have an orderly sergeant to call on him with positive orders that the

Adjutant should attend the General in haste that then he should make an excuse to the Gentn suspected as a spy. and leave him alone about half an hour.—This was done. and in this Interval as was suspected the Spy, took a Copy of the returns, and next morning went off with them to New York.— This Convinced Genl Howe that we were too strong to be attacked & saved us thro' the Winter.

A Col Luce who was taken Prisoner at Elizabethtown was confined to a House in Morris Town., in a family disaffected to our cause, on his parole. —He found out our real situation and obtained full acct. of our weakness. and. indeed returns of the Army. Artillery &c with our poverty, sickness &c &c according to the truth. with these, expecting to make his fortune He broke his parole & run off to New York. He was introduced to Genl Howe and with great zeal communicated the whole secret Genl Howe called for the returns brought by the spy; and then in the severest tone, charged Col Luce with joining the Rebels in endeavouring to impose upon him and draw him out into the Country. and threatened to hang him up at the first tree, Luce was terrified beyond description as Howe produced copies of the returns from the American Brigadiers obtained in such a manner that there could be no doubt. Luce was glad to escape with his life. Mortified and chagrined with having broken his Parole & at last dissapointed and treated with contempt & great Severity, he took to drink & killed himself by it in the end.

MOTION MADE IN CONGRESS TO EXECUTE LORD
CORNWALLIS, IN RETALIATION FOR THE MUR-
DER OF COLONEL HAINES, AND CRUELTIES
COMMITTED ON PRISONERS IN PHILADELPHIA.

TREATMENT OF PRISONERS IN PHILADELPHIA
JANY AND FEB 1778

Various Reports having reached us with regard
to the Extreme Sufferings of our Prisoners in
Philadelphia, I was directed by the Commander in
Chief to make particular inquiry into the truth.
After sometime I obtained full Information of their
Sufferings. It was proved by some Militia of good
Character, that on being taken they were put under
care of the General's Guard & kept 4 & 5 days
without the least food. That on the 5th day they
were taken into the Provost. where a small quantity of Raw Pork was given to them. One of
their number seized and devoured it with so much
eagerness, that he immediately dropped down dead
—that the Provost Marshal used to sell their provisions & leave them to starve, as he did their Allowance of Wood.—I recd information of a British
Officer. who confided in my Integrity—that he
happened in the Provost. just at the time the provost Marshal (Cunningham) was looking up the
Prisoners. He had ordered them from the Yard
into the House. Some of them being ill with the
Dysentery, could scarcely walk. and for not coming
faster he would beat them with his Rattan.—One
being in the necessary delayed longer than the rest,
on his coming up Cunningham gave him a blow

with one of the large Keys. of the Goal—which
killed him on the Spot; The Officer exceedingly
affected with the sight, went next day and lodged
a formal Complaint of the Murder with Genl
Howe's Aid. After waiting some days; and not discovering any measures taken for the tryal of Cunningham, he again went to head Quarters & requested to see the General. but was refused. he
repeated his Complaint to his Aid, and told him if
this past unpunished. it would become disreputable
to wear a british Uniform. No notice being taken,
the Officer determined to furnish one privately
with the means of proof of the Facts. so that Genl
Washington might remonstrate to Genl Howe on
the subject.—I reported them with the other Testimony I had collected to Genl W—— He accordingly wrote in pretty strong Terms to Genl Howe
and fixed a day, when if he did not receive a satis-
factory answer, he would retaliate on the Prisoners
in his Custody.—On the day, he recd an answer,
from Genl Howe. acknowledging that on Examination, he found that Cunningham had sold the
Prisoners Rations publicly in the Market. That
he had therefor removed him from the Charge of
the Prisoners & appointed Mr Henry H. Ferguson in his place.—This gave us great pleasure as
we knew Mr Ferguson to be a Gentn of Character
& great Humanity and the issue justified our Expectations—But to our great surprise Mr Cunningham was only removed from the Charge of the Prisoners in Philadelphia & sent to that of New York,

Soon after this, great complaints being made of our Prisoners being likely to perish for want of Cloathing & Blankets, having been mostly stripped & robbed of their Cloaks when taken. Application was made for permission to purchase, (with the Provisions which the British Wanted) Blankets & cloathing, which should be used only by the Prisoners while in Confinement.—This was agreed to, as we were informed by our own Agent as well as by the British Commissioner—Provisions were accordingly attempted to be sent in, When Genl Howe pretending to ignorance in the business, forbid the provisions to be admitted. or the Blankets to be purchased.—On this I gave notice to the British commissary that after a certain day. they must provide food for their prisoners South West of New Jersey, & to be sent in from their lines. as they should no longer be allowed to purchase provisions with us. The line drawn. arose from our being at liberty to purchase in New York,— This made a great noise, when Genl Howe on receiving Genl Robertsons letter from New York before mentioned. urging the propriety of the measures. issued an order that every Person in Philadelphia who had a Blanket to sell or to spare. should bring them into the Kings Stores.—When this was done. he then gave my agent permission to purchase Blankets & cloathing in the City of Philadelphia.—On my agent attempting it, he found every Blanket in the City. purchased by the agents for the Army. so that not a Blanket could be had.—My Agent knowing the necessities of our Prisoners. immediately employed persons in every part of the city, and. before Genl Howe could discover his omission, purchased up every piece of Flannel. he could meet with & mad it up into a kind of Blanket. which answered our purpose—

Lord Cornwallis while Commanding in South Carolina had behaved with great Cruelty to the Citizens, in the Opinion of the delegates from that State, and was specially charged with the Murder of Col Haines, under pretext of Martial Law.— This enraged the Gentlemen from the Southward, & particularly a Mr. Middleton and soon after Lord Cornwallis' Capture, a Motion was made in Congress, that General Washington should cause his Lordship to be executed in retaliation of Col Haines and other cruelties committed by him— This motion was strongly advocated by a very large party in the House. and the prospect of its success greatly alarmed many moderate Members of Congress.—Mr Duane & Myself opposed it with all our powers. as contrary to all good faith, having entered into a Capitulation with him, after the facts committed, & having knowledge of them.— That it would Expose our Commander in Chief to the necessity of resigning his Command or forfeiting his Honor & Reputation &c &c &c. The debate continued several Day's and with great difficulty we succeeded in putting a negative on it, by a small Majority

WASHINGTON AND CONGRESS DECIDE TO EXECUTE
CAPTAIN ASGILL OF THE BRITISH ARMY, IN
RETALIATON FOR THE FOUL MURDER OF CAP-
TAIN HUDDY, BUT HIS LIFE IS SPARED AT THE
REQUEST OF THE KING AND QUEEN OF FRANCE.

In the Year —— Govr Franklin as the head of
the Refugees. sent out a party of Refugees into
the County of Monmouth New Jersey, & took
Capt Huddy prisoner—By their particular Orders
he was hanged in a very insulting a cruel manner,
under pretense of retaliation for a Person who was
shot in the Act of running away from his Guard.
—This made a great noise in our camp & thro'out
the State—Genl Washington saw the necessity of
not suffering so great an Act of Barbarity contrary to all the Rules of civilized Warfare, to pass
unnoticed—He therefore sent immediate orders to
Lancaster where a number of British Officers
(Prisoners) were kept. to draw lotts for one who
should be made an Example of. by being hanged
in retaliation for Huddy, unless he obtained full
satisfaction by the Enemy sending out the Author
of the inhuman Act.—Notice of this was given to
Congress. who readily approved the measure—
Notice was also given to the British Commander
in New York The Lott was drawn & it fell on
Capt. Asgill Son of Sir Charles Asgill. He was
accordingly sent to General Washington at Moores

Town: a number of Officers of his Corps attended him, who were allowed No remonstrates to their General—The British immediately ordered the Officer commanding the Party. to be arrested & tryed by a Court Marshal, and Notice of this was formally given to Genl Washington with a request that Asgils Execution might be delayed till the determination of the Court Marshal was known——The sitting of the Court was drawn out to a great length, when finally the Prisoner was found not guilty of Murder with Malice prepense and a copy of the Proceedings were sent to Genl Washington & by him to Congress. It clearly appeared from the Testimony that the Prisoner acted under orders from the Board of Refugees, of Which Govr Franklin was President. and that tho' the Prisoner might be entitled to the Acquittal. that yet Govr Franklin was the Culprit & should have been punished.

Congress took the matter under full consideration, during which Genl Sir Guy Carleton arrived at New York with the Title of Commander in Chief & the Preliminary Articles of Peace were anounced.—Genl Washington then wrote to Congress. that he had first proposed the retaliation on Capt. Asgil. as an Act of Mercy on the whole. to put a stop to the Enemy destroying the lives of our Citizens, in future as they had done in times past, That he had determined to carry it into execution. not being satisfied with the result of the

Court Marshal. But that unexpectedly the preliminary Articles of Peace had wholly changed the ground—The Execution of an innocent person ought to have an object in view to prevent the unnecessary shedding of Blood—That the example now could not have any effect. as there would be nothing for it to operate upon &c &c. that therefore he should stay the Execution of Capt. Asgil. without an express order from Congress to the Contrary—

A very large Majority of Congress were determined on his Execution, and a Motion was made for a resolution positively ordering his immediate Execution—Mr Duane & Myself considering the reasons assigned by the Commander in Chief conclusive, made all the opposition in our power, we urged every Argument that the peculiarity of the Case suggested and spent three days in warm debate. during which more ill blood appeared in the House. than I had seen. Near the Close of the third day, when every argument was exausted, without any appearance of success, the matter was brought to a close by the Question being ordered to be taken.—I again rose and told the House. that in so important a Case the life of an innocent Person was concerned. we had (Tho in a small minority) exerted ourselves to the utmost of our Power, we had acquitted of Conscience and wished our hands clear from the blood of that young man. That we saw his fate was sealed. That now we had nothing to do but request that the proceedings should appear

without Doors, as being equal to the occasion.
and the world should know that we had conducted
the measure with a serious Solemnity That great
warmth had been occasioned, some harsh language
had taken place The Minds of Gentn had been irri-
tated, I therefore moved that the Question should
be put off till the next morning, on the Minority
giving their Words, that they would not say
another word on the subject but the Question should be taken in the first place, after the
meeting as of course.—This was unanimously
agreed to.—The next morning as soon as the
minutes were read ; the President anounced a letter from the Commander in Chief—On its being
read. it stated the Rect of a letter from the
King & Queen of France & enclosing one from
Mrs Asgil the Mother of Capt Asgil to the Queen.,
that on the whole were enough to move the heart
of a Savage.—The subject was asking the life of
young Asgil.—This operated like an electrical
shock. Each member looking on his neighbor in
surprise, as if saying here is unfair play. It was
suspected to be some scheme of the Minority.—
The President was interrogated, The Cover of
the letter was called for. The General's Signature
was examined. In short. it looked so much like
something supernatural that even the minority,
who were so much pleased with it. could scarcely
think it real. After being fully convinced of the
integrity of the Transaction. a motion was made

that the life of Capt Asgil should be given as a
Compliment to the King of France. This was
unanimously carried.—On which it was moved
that the Commander in Chief should remand
Capt Asgil to his Quarters at Lancaster. To this
I objected. That as we considered Capt Asgil's
Life as forfeited & and we had given him to the King
of France. he was now a free man. and therefor
I moved that he should be immediately returned
into New York; without Exchange. This also was
unanimously adopted, and thus we got clear of
shedding innocent Blood. by a wonderful inter-
vention of Providence. Capt Asgil soon sailed
for England, and on his arrival he behaved without
any sense of obligation for his escape. suffering
the most false & injurious accts of his liberation
to be published in all the News Papers. without an
attempt to contradict them—Indeed I found generally that the British Officers did not think themselves bound to keep their word. or perform acts
of common gratitude & generosity with rebels. In
this charge I refer to those who were Prisoners,
with us. but I must here except Col. afterwards
Sir Archibald Campbell. who behaved in every instance as a man of strict honor & unbounded be-
nevolence. Tho' treated by us, Thro' a Mistake, the
worst of any Prisoner during the war.

Among our first exchange a number of the
British Prisoners (Officers) in Connecticut, could
not repay the money that had been advanced to

them for their support, without which they could
not be liberated,—Loath to keep them Prisoners,
I accepted in lieu of money, their Bills drawn on
their friends in London. These I sent to New
York for sale.—General Howo refused permission
for selling them.—I then had them remitted to
London.—They were all protested but one—And
the Person on whom one was drawn by Ensign or
Lieut Noland, annexed to the protest an original
letter from Noland to him. advising of his having drawn, but requesting him not to pay the Bill,
as he did not think himself bound to keep faith
with rebels.—After the Peace I catched this Gent
in America and made him pay it, with full interest.

In like Circumstances, a Major Edminston was
Exchanged who owed forty Pounds, I left him go
on a Solemn promise to send the money immediately on his arrival in Philadelphia. not hearing
from him for a considerable time I wrote to him
upbraiding him with his breach of Promise. He
gave me no Answer. I then wrote to the Commissary of Prisoners remonstrating on this Conduct. and assuring him that it would prevent (in
future) any acts of kindness. of this sort towards
Gentn in distress—He answered that he showed
my letter to Edminston but recd no satisfaction
from him—and he never paid it.

WASHINGTON REFUSES TO PUNISH A KNOWN TRAITOR, WITHOUT EVIDENCE.

SUPRISE OF GENL LINCOLN AT BOUND BROOK

In 1777 Genl Lincoln. was surprised at the Dawn of Day in his Quarters at Bound Brook. by Lord Cornwallis. who had marched from Brunswick passed his out Centinels captured or destroyed his main guard, and was at the Genls Quarters before he knew anything of it. He had but just time to escape out of a back door. Several men were killed and one or two pieces of ordnance taken. It was sometime a mystery how this had been effected with so much secrecy. till I was well informed by a Gentn of note who was with the Enemy at Brunswick. that a certain Farmer whose name he mentioned and who lived in the midst of our Camp had communicated to Lord Cornwallis our Countersign, by which he had accomplished his intentions, My spirit was very much aroused ags this Traitor and with great zeal I went to Genl Washington with the information, stating the substance of it. but keeping back the name of my informant; as he had assured me his life depended on my prudence & faithfulness to him; I urged the Genl, (to give) orders to sieze the Culprit without delay & make an Example of him. The Genl did not immediately answer me. on which I repeated my request.

He then said. did not you tell me that the life of your informant depended on your secrecy,—would you take up a Citizen & confine him without letting him know his crime or his accuser.— No—let him alone for the present: watch him carefully. and if you can catch him in any other crime. so as to confront him by witnesses. we will then punish him severely.——My mortification was very great. to think. that I who had entered the Army to watch the Military & preserve the civil rights of my fellow citizens. should be so reproved by a Military man, who was so interested in having acted otherwise I recd it as a severe lecture on my own imprudence

THE MANNER IN WHICH ELIAS BOUDINOT SUC-
CEEDED IN GETTING CONGRESS TO PAY HIM
BACK THE MONEY HE ADVANCED TO FEED
AND CLOTHE CONTINENTAL SOLDIERS, WHO
WERE PRISONERS OF WAR.

MY ACCT. WITH CONGRESS

When I found every application to obtain hard
Money from Congress for the Cloathing of our
Prisoners in vain, I waited on Genl Washington,
and proposed my resignation as my Character was
at stake, having (on the promise of the Secret
Committee to yield me every necessary aid)
pledged myself to the Officers in Confinement
that they should be regularly supplied with every
necessary, but they now suffered more than ever—
In much distress & with tears in his eyes; he assured me that if he was deserted by the Gentn of
the Country, he should despair. He could not do
every thing, He was Genl. Quarter Master & Commissary. Every thing fell on him & he was unequal to the task. He gave me the most positive
Engagement that if I would contrive any mode
for their support & Comfort. he would confirm it as
far as was in his Power——On this I told him
that I knew of but one way. & that was to borrow
money on my own private Security He assured
me that in case I did. and was not reimbursed by
Congress. he would go an Equal sharer with me

in the loss. I then formed the plan of obliging Genl Burgoyne to pay hard money for the support of the British Prisoners whom we supplied with daily rations. and in the meantime proceeded to borrow money or take Goods in New York on my own Credit.—Thus I furnished 300 Officers with a handsome suit of Cloaths each. and 1100 men with a plain suit, Found them Blankets, Shirts &c. and added to their provisions found by the British a full half ration of Bread & Beef pr day. for upwards of 15 months Part of this I supplied by sending Wheat & Flour to New York. & selling them for hard money. under leave from Genl Robertson.——Sometime in the beginning of the year 1778 Congress Recd. from Genl Burgoyne nearly 40,000 Dollars in hard money. In the beginning of 1778 I was chosen a Member of Congress, but continued in the Army till June. When Genl Washington knowing that I was near Thirty Thousand Dollars in advance for the Prisoners. urged me to go and take my seat in Congress. where I might get some of the hard money recd from Genl Burgoyne. before it was all expended, for if it was once gone. I should be totally ruined I accordingly left the Army & found Congress on their return from York Town in Pennsylvania ; after the British had evacuated the City of Philadelphia.— I applied to the Chamber of Acct. and with Great difficulty got my acct settled. A very large Ballance was found in my favor, and a warrant ordered

for 15000 Dolls Continental and a report made that
I had actually advanced the Cash, and there was
upwards of Ten Thousand Pounds hard money
that I yet owed.—I urged the appointment of a
Committee of Congress to an examination of these
expenditures & to report upon them.—Richard.
Henry Lee & Wm Duer were accordingly appointed. and after a full Examination reported the
sum of Twenty Six Thousand Six hundred &
Sixty Six Dollars & $\frac{2}{3}$ °/ in specie. for which they
recommended a warrant to be immediately issued.
On Considering the report Mr Dana from Massachusetts. & Mr Merchant from Rhode Island opposed the report of the Committee with great insolence, insisting that as Mr Boudinot had taken up
this money at the instance of Genl Washington.
without the approbation of Congress. he had no
right to be paid but in Continental money as other
Creditors of Congress.—After much altercation I
got up & informed the House that I had borrowed
this money on my private Credit, in the City of
New York.—That I should never ask the House
for the payment of it again—That I should on my
return home, sell what property I had & pay as
far as that would go, and then publish to the world
why I was insolvent for the Balance.—But also
informed the House, that even to that moment, our
prisoners in New York were fed & cloathed on my
Private Credit.—That I would immediately send
orders, to stop farther issues to them on my acct.

in 10 days, and desired provision might be made for these unhappy people after the expiration of that time, on which they went to other business without doing anything on the Report.

I sent orders to my Agent in New York, and all further issues were stopped accordingly.

The Latter end of July. I recd a very affecting letter from my Agent, painting the destitution of the Prisoners in so striking a manner, and the death of several more than had been usual; That I could not longer persist in my determination of silence on the subject. Having recd this letter in Congress, I rose with tears in my eyes, and reminding them of my former promise begged leave to break thro' it, so far as to read the letter which I did.— On this Mr Duer, (a man of much feeling) rose and in a speech of more than half an hour declaimed so severely agst the ungrateful Conduct of the House. that a unanimous vote immediately passed for a warrant in my favor £10.000 in specie. which was immediately sent to New York.

SCARCITY OF POWDER AT BOSTON.

When our Army lay before Boston in 1775, our Powder was so nearly Expended, That General Washington told me that he had not more than Eight Rounds. a Man, Altho' he had then near 14 miles of line to guard, and that he dare not fire an Evening or Morning Gun. In this situation one of the Committee of Safety for Massachusetts, who was privy to the whole secret, deserted and went over to Genl Gage, and discovered our poverty to him. The fact was so incredible, That Genl Gage treated it as a stratagem of war, and the informant as a spy: or coming with the express purpose of deceiving him & drawing his Army into a snare, by which means we were saved from having our Quarters beaten up.—I was the chairman of the Committee of safety at Elizabeth Town, and had about six or Seven Quarter Casks of Powder, which on urgent application from Genl Washington were sent to Boston. with what could be spared from New York.

The History of the Exchange of General
Charles Lee, who was Captured by the
British, Describing his Indelicate Behav-
ior in General Washington's House, and
Narrating his Infamous Tirade Against
Washington, and his Ridiculous Proposi-
tion to Congress.

Exchange of Genl Lee &c &c &c

In Dec 1776. Genl Lee being taken prisoner at
his Quarters at. Baskinridge in the County of Som-
erset (New Jersey) about 4 Miles to the left of his
Troops towards the Enemy, by his own extreme
negligence & folly, was removed. (after the British
Cantonments were beaten up. at Trenton & Princeton) to New York & confined to a handsome House.
under the Care of 4 or 5 field Officers, who lived
with him & kept a genteel Table.—In this situation
he sent to congress, requesting a Committee of their
Body, might be sent over to him as he had something
of consequence to communicate to them. and for
the purpose sent Genl Howe's safe conduct, for their
Security. This congress very justly refused &
treated the application with deserved contempt.
In January 1778. I was sent by Genl Washington
over to New York (with consent of Genl Howe)
to examine into the actual Situation of our Prisoners, and had orders to pay particular attention to
Genl Lee, and accomplish his exchange if possible.

The Morning after my Arrival, I waited on Genl
Lee who received me with great pleasure indeed,
and asked me to Breakfast with him the next day.
—This I did in company with the Officers who had
the care of him, and was treated with Great politeness & Affibility When Breakfast was over, Genl
Lee asked me up into his Room.—He soon began
to complain very heavily of the treatment he had
recd from Congress, in not complying with his request.—I told him that I thought they had done
perfectly right; not to trust any of their members
within the British Lines; on such an Errand. He
replied that he had obtained a safe passport for
them from Genl Howe, and they might have come
with the utmost safety. I then asked him what
end could have been answered by their coming.—
Sir said he, I had discovered the whole plan of the
Summer's Campaign on the part of the British, and
would have disclosed the whole to the Committee,
by which Congress might have obviated all their
Measures, for Mr Boudinot it is in vain for Congress to expect to withstand British Troops in the
Field.—I answered that he must now be convinced
that without his Information they had been with-
stood and that the Campaign had passed over, and
the Enemy had gained no great advantage with all
their force and strength. But (I continued) General will you answer me explicitly, did you inform
General Howe that this was your design. he answered by no means. Then Genl. said I, do tell

me what reasons did you assign to Genl Howe for so extraordinary a Measure, as sending for three members of Congress to be permitted to enter a garrisoned town. and to confer with their own General, a Prisoner of War. To this he would give no answer. But immediately began to urge the impossibility of our troops under such an Ignorant Commander in Chief, ever withstanding British Grenadiers & Light Infantry—And immediately put his hand into his Pocket & pulled out a manuscript of 2 or 3 sheets and said he charged it to me. to hearken to what he would read to me. and as soon as I returned to Jersey. That I would repair to Congress & not leave them. till I had prevailed upon them to adopt his Plan. He then read his manuscript, which was a laboured Argument to prove the impossibilty of making head agt the British Army. and that therefor we should set it down as certain. that in the next Campaign we must be compleatly defeated—He therefor urged. that congress would immediately have a strong fortress Built at Pittsburgh and also several hundred Boats, that they would order all the Riches of the Country to be sent there with the Old Men. Women. & Children, and that when they found themselves driven there. that Congress &c &c might take Boat & go down the Ohio to the Spanish Territory. for Protection—The whole of this plan struck me in so absurd a light, added to the impropriety of reading such a thing to me who he knew was on my

parole of honor. within an Enemys Lines. (for altho'
it had not been formally regarded, yet I considered
myself. more firmly bound, if Possible. than if it
had been expressly given) that I could not but en-
tertain the greatest Jealousy of the Integrity of
Genl Lee—I answered without hesitation that I
could not take any such message to Congress from
him; or any other, without the knowledge of the
British Generals.—That I thought he had been very
wrong to attempt any such, Communication to me,
knowing my Situation and that I should consider
myself as having not heard it.—That I wondered
at his prudence. in keeping such a writing in his
pockett, as the Discovery of it in his Pockett & in
his hand writing might cost him his life—He then.
waived the Business & I left him.—I endeavoured
to negotiate his exchange, and it was agreed (Hy-
pothetically) that it should take place for Major
Genl Prescott. subject to Genl Howe's approbation
Genl Howe objected, and ordered Genl Lee round
by Sea to Philadelphia. that he might be exchanged
under his own eye.—Genl Lee (abhoring the Sea)
applied to me by letter & most earnestly requested
that he might be permitted to go thro' New Jersey,
under the care of a British Officer, to which Genl
Washington consented, and he accordingly went
to Philadelphia. but no consent was obtained to
the exchange—In the spring of 1778 a proposition
was made by both parties for a partial Exchange
of Prisoners, and I was ordered to Germantown to

meet the British Commissory. to attempt the business. When I was setting off from Camp, Genl Washington called me into his Room, and in the most earnest manner intreated of me, if I wished to gratify him. that I wou.d obtain the Exchange of Genl Lee, for he never was more wanted by him. than at the present moment, and desired that I would not suffer trifles to prevent it. I accordingly went, and made a pretty considerable Exchange of Prisoners, but quite new propositions were made for the Exchange of Genl Lee, which neither the General or myself had ever thought of, after reducing the Terms to as favourable a Scale as I thought right, I agreed to it on Condition, that if General Washington was not pleased with the new plan. and Notice was given of his refusal within 24 Hours. The Exchange was to be void, without any charge of Failure on my part. I arrived at head Quaters about 6 O'clock P. M. and going into the General began to tell him of my success—When he interrupted me with much Eagerness and asked me if I had exchanged Genl Lee, I informed him of what had been done; he replied sit down at this Table, and write a letter informing of my Confirmation of the Exchange & send one of my Horse Guards immediately to the Enemies lines with it, I assured him that next day would be time enough. but he insisted on its being immediately done. and I sent him accordingly, fixing the next day but one for Genl Lee's coming out to us.—When the day arrived the greatest preparations were made for his reception all the principal Officers of the Army were drawn up in two lines, advanced of the Camp about 2 miles towards the Enemy.—Then the troops with the inferior Officers formed a line quite to head Quarters. All the Music of the Army attended. The General with a great number of principal Officers. and their Suites, rode about four miles on the road towards Philadelphia and waited till Genl Lee appeared.—Gen Washington dismounted & recd Gen Lee as if he had been his brother.—He passed thro' the lines of Officers & the Army. who all paid him the highest military Honors to Head Quarters, where Mrs Washington was. and there he was entertained with an Elegant Dinner, and the Music Playing the whole time.—A Room was assigned him. Back of Mrs Washington's Sitting Room. and all his Baggage was stowed in it.   The next morning he lay very late. and Breakfast was detained for him.   When he came out. he looked as dirty as if he had been in the Street all night. soon after I discovered that he had brought a miserable dirty hussy with him from Philadelphia (a British Sergeants Wife) and had actually taken her into his Room by a Back Door and she had slept with him that night.

Genl Washington gave him the command of the Right Wing of the Army. but before he took charge of it, he requested leave to go to Congress at York Town ; which was readily granted. Before he went I had an interview with him.—He expressed himself under the greatest obligations to me, and assured me that he never should forget my kindness. But wished exceedingly to know. if I had made his communication to Congress & what was their opinion of it, I assured him that I had not. and if he was wise he would say nothing upon the subject. He said he was going to Congress for that purpose and he never would not rest till it was done, and he was more than ever convinced that nothing else could save us, That he found the Army in a worse situation than he expected and that General Washington was not fit to command a Sergeant's Guard.—This mortified me greatly. after all the kindness shown him by Genl Washington—My Jealousy of him was greatly confirmed, and I began to interrogate him about his reception at Philadelphia and immediately brought about the question wether he had seen Genl Howe. He told me that he had been closeted by him the Evening but one, before he left the City I urged him to tell me the substance of the Conversation that passed between them, He told me that Genl Howe began to talk upon the Claim of Independence by the Americans. That he thought it one of the most absurd & hopeless expectations that could enter into the mind of sensible Men; And as for you, Lee, says he, What in the Devil could get into you to be so crazy, who ought to know better. Lee answered that He

thought it a very wise measure and that if it had
not been done, the Americans would have been
without excuse.—The General replied ; why what
end can it answer, do you think there is the most
distant possibility of their succeeding, to which
Genl Lee, replied., They were perfectly right.   In
case of a Treaty what have they to give up., for
what may they insist on receiving, had they made
no claim to Independence.—O' Sir said the General. if that is all they mean by it. it may be proper
enough.—but I supposed they aimed at insisting on
a separation from the Mother Country.—but in this
View it may be well enough : and as he said they
parted—But General Howe sent him a store of
Wine, Spirit, Porter, &c &c to take out with him,
but the British Soldiers finding out, that it was
Stored in the Cellar of the House where he lodged ;
broke into it the night before he came away, &
stole the whole of it.——All this increased my
suspicions of Genl Lee exceedingly, and I watched
him with a Jealous Eye.

He went to Congress, and as I was afterwards
informed. he applied to Congress for a committee
to meet and confer with him.   The President Mr
Laurence was directed to this Service, to whom
Genl Lee communicated his Plan, which disgusted
Mr Laurence so greatly that he would not even
report it to Congress.—This lessened the General
so greatly in the Eyes of Congress. that they never
paid much respect to him afterwards —— He

returned to the army and took command of the right wing—He immediately began to rebel agt Genl Washington & to quarrel with the Marquise La Fayette He assured himself that Genl Washington was ruining the whole cause. that he was looking forward. to the British evacuating Philadelphia & going to New York, and of course strengthing his left., while the right was totally unguarded But Lee said that the Enemy would press over to Chester & come suddenly on their right wing and we should be wholly overthrown, He said he urged this in council, but that he had been overruled & there fore was no longer accountable.—When the British Army actually passed thro' Jersey & Genl Washington by his great precaution, had advanced two Brigades towards the Delaware, and therefor overtook the British at freehold, Genl Lee was greatly mortified & at first refused to take the Command of the advanced Party & it was given to the Marquiss La Fayette. But on finding that the advanced Army was reinforced & raised to a very respectable Command, he insisted on the Command, and to keep peace it was given to him.

Genl Lee accordingly came up with Genl Clinton near freehold Court House. and a skirmish took place.—Genl Lee had considerable Military Knowledge & did very well on a small scale. but I have no doubt that whenever any thing on a very large scale struck him. that a partial Lunacy took place.

His behaviour this morning discovered this state of mind, which might have been increased from the peculiarity of his situation and his exalted idea of the prowness of British Troops.—In the midst of the Engagement he rode up to a Lt Coll of my Acquaintance who had a single field piece firing and called to him. " Coll have you seen anything improper in my Conduct this morning ? The Coll (who had been convinced of something wrong in the Genl all the Morning, yet not choosing to acknowledge it) answered, no by no means.—well then said the General, do you remember that. Such an Extraordinary question from a Commander in Chief of a division, under such Extraordinary Circumstances, is full proof that he must have felt something unusual in himself.

The issue was that he was beat, and had not Genl Washington have come up on a lucky moment & turned the fortune of the Day, It might have been fatal to America.

The Taking of Major Andre.

Major Andre. who was Adjutant General of the
British Army., having entered into a correspond-
ence with General Benedict Arnold, who then
commanded the Important post of West Point on
the North River, which was estimated as the key
to the state of New York, and indeed all the upper
country, in which great part of the New England
States were also greatly interested, soon ripend it
into an actual communication for delivering up
that Post to the British on Terms of personal
emolument to Arnold. The fear of detection, led
the American General to propose a personal meeting on the Shore of the North River at some distance below West Point & without the out posts,
that matters might be finally settled, and the
Treason be compleated.—Andre being greatly
elated with his success entered warmly into the
measure, and Genl Clinton the Commander in
Chief of the British Army, recieved the proposal
with great Expectation, and immediately provided
Andre (to whom he was much attached & had
made him one of his particular confidents) with a
20 Gun ship to go up the River as if to Command
that part of the River. In the Evening the Ship
came to Anchor. and after night (Andre) was landed
privately on the main land ; where he met Arnold.,

them that he was ; and by taking him into their
officer, they would know it to be true and he would
reward them for it., on their doubting. he pulled
out a gold Watch & said by that they might know
he was not a Common Man. They then told him
if that was the Case, he was their Prisoner for they
were Americans, and therefore insisted on search-
ing him.—Andre finding himself in this disagreeable predicament, began to beg, and assuring them
that he was only a Citizen of New York, who had
important family business in the Country, had
gone to finish it, and was returning.—That his
capture could not be of service to them. but would
be a great injury to him, and if they would release
him he would engage to return them, safely delivered in any private place on the lines they should
name any reasonable Quantity of British Goods
they should desire.—They answered : You a British Officer & not a common man surely you could
do more than this for your liberty, we are poor
Militia Soldiers & you a great Officer—Andre then
took out his Watch & offered that into the Bar-
gain : They repeated that his liberty was worth
more than a gold watch. & if he was a British
Officer he could give more still.—He then pulled
out a purse of gold. & offered them both,—They
then told him he must be a fool. do you not see
that you. & your Watch & your money, are all in
our power ; no we are Americans : and all that you
are worth could not tempt us to release you;

Therefore immediately submit to be searched.—accordingly he turned out his Pockets.—finding nothing material, they ordered him to pull off his Boots.—He pulled off one. but said he would go no further & refused to pull off the other, on which they tripped up his heels, and on pulling off his Boot, out came all his papers.—They immediately carried him into their Post and delivered him with all the Papers to their Officer Lt Coll Jameson.—This Conduct in these three Men, as Militia being generally of low Character & not very famous for their strict attention to the Property of the Inhabitants on the Lines. certainly proved an exception to the general rule.

The Officer was Thunder Struck on finding the Papers in the hand writing of General Arnold; and that the Plan was to deliver up the Fort with General Washington while at dinner. Andre said his name was Anderson. Jameson's positive orders as Commanding this out Post; was to give instant Notice to General Arnold, of every thing that should turn up of an extraordinary Nature and had light horse stationed with him for the purpose. What to do at first, he did not know.—But calling a soldier he put much Confidence in, gave him a letter to General Arnold, acquainting him with the outlines of the Capture of a Mr Anderson, going into New York, and set it off according to the letter of his orders ; but gave secret orders to the Soldier. to lame his Horse by the way. and to be detained by it, for

24 Hours. He then sent another off to ride Post
& meet General Washington on his return from
Connecticut. with the Papers found on Andre.
The Horseman took the Road General Washington
went, not knowing that he made it a rule never to
go & return by the same road. By this means he
missed the General, but heard of his return at a
cross road and the Horseman sent to Arnold arrived at General Arnold's Quarters : a short time
before General Washington, as soon as Arnold
recd the letter he sprang out of his Room, Just
looked into the Room where his wife was ; and told
her that he must bid her farewell forever, and ran
down to the fort., and got on board his barge, and
ordered the Bargemen to row him down the River
—General Washington arrived soon after., and en-
quiring at Arnold's Quarters for the General. was
told that he had just gone to the Fort., General
Washington rode immediately down. and being put
over to the fort. he found that the General was not
there, but the Officer of the Day, attended him
round the Works.—Arnold not appearing General
Washington expressed some resentment at his not
attending him. and suddenly returned to his Horse,
he was scarcely mounted, when the Horseman appeared with the Papers taken on Andre—As soon
as he had read the letter. & cast his Eye over the
Papers. he put spur to his Horse. & rode to Arnold's
Door. and called out his Aid Du Camp. and drawing his Pistol from his holster. solemnly declared

he would blow his brains out. if he did not instantly tell him where Arnold was.—The extreme fright of the Aid & his whole appearance convinced the General of his innocence, as he could tell him no more. than that on recieving a Horseman from an Outpost; he had in great terror left the House & gone alone to the Fort. The General instantly ordered Coll Hamilton to ride post to the Fort. at Verplank's Point opposite Stony Point, and order the Fort to fire on the Barge; taking it for granted that he was gone down the River, Hamilton arrived just as the fort was paying the usual Compliment to the General's Barge.—Hamilton instantly pointed the Guns, and fired on the Barge. Arnold rose and with a Pistol in each hand, swore he would put the first man to death who should stop his oar. and soon passed out of reach of the Fort.

Andre was sent to Head Quarters and put under the Care of a subaltern Officer and a strong Guard —In the night Andre acknowledge to the Officer that he was Adjutant General of the British Army. That he found it in vain to cover himself with a fictitious name and. therefore. should appear in his real Character. The Officer was so alarmed, that he slept not a moment, but in the morning communicated this Intelligence to Head Quarters.—Coll Hamilton, who had seen Andre was sent to him, and knew him to be the man—General Washington out of respect to his Character, instead of a more summary proceeding called a Council of General

Officers, of whom La Fayette & Steuben were two.,
who were to enquire into the facts & the Crime
of the Prisoner.—Andre finding himself unexpectedly treated with so much propriety & kindness,
confessed every fact, and appeared only solicit-
ous to free himself from any suspicion of being a
Spy, or having voluntarily acted unbecoming his
Character.—The Council found him guilty & that
he was worthy of Death. His execution was determined on, and the day fixed. But on a letter
from Genl Clinton, he was reprieved for a few
days.—The News of Andre's Capture greatly
alarmed & affected the Army, and Andre's fate
was sincerely deplored, and some compassionate
minds, were ready to wish for his pardon, But as
soon as the reprieve was known ; and it was suggested by some discontented Persons that this reprieve was prepatory to a pardon & Discharge ; but
a universal alarm took place.—The Officers generally declared that if they were not to be protected
ags such traitorous Conduct ; it was time to leave
the Army, That if they were to be exposed to ex-
ternal Spys & internal machinations, and no punish-
ment inflicted on them, who were taken and proved
guilty, there would be no safety in the Camp and
resignation was the only protection.—Tho these
were their sentiments, they were only murmured
from Tent to Tent.—a few days convinced them
that they had a Commander in Chief who knew how
to make his Compassion for the unfortunate & his

duty to those who depended upon him, for protection to harmonize and Influence his Conduct.—He treated Major Andre with the greatest tenderness, while he carried the Sentence of the Council into strict Execution according to the laws of War— At New York when the first account of Andre's Capture & Condemnation arrived, the Officers & Citizens laughed at the idea that the Rebels would dare to execute the Adjutant General of the British Army, but if it should take place, that Vengeance on every rebel should be taken seven fold.—But when it was known that Andre was no more, General Clinton shut himself up for 3 days & every one at the Coffee House & other Public Places. hung their heads, and scarcely an observation relative to it, escaped their lips.—Arnold was made a Brigadier General, and tho' great Expectations were formed of his invitations to the American Soldiers & Citizens to Join him agt the Rebellion of their Country, it is generally believed that scarcely a soldier ever deserted or a Citizen Joined him.—He lived dispised & disregarded, and died unlamented & unnoticed—Thus having rec'd the general reward of a Traitor to his Country.

GENERAL WASHINGTON'S PASSAGE TO NEW YORK
FROM ELIZABETH TOWN, WITH COMMITTEE OF
CONGRESS, WHEN FIRST CHOSEN. PRESID'T OF
THE UNITED STATES, 23RD APRIL 1789.

Extract of letter written back to Elizabeth Town.

If it was in my power, I would wish to give you
an adequate account of the proceedings of the Citizens of this metropolis, on the approach, and at the
reception of their beloved Chief, when he arrived
here yesterday.—I cannot do it Justice, and therefore should not attempt it, had I not so much vanity
as to think you will be in some measure gratified,
by its coming thro this chance however imperfect.

You must have observed, with what a propitious
Gale, we left my beloved shore and glided with
steady Motion across New Ark Bay, the waters
seeming to rejoice in bearing so precious a burthen
over its placid Bosom—the distant appearance of
the Troops, The Militia in Uniform we had left behind and their regular firings, added much to our
pleasure. When we drew near to the mouth of
the Kills, a number of Boats with a great variety
of superb Flags came up to us, and dropped in

our wake—Soon after we opened the Bay., General Knox and several Gentn of distinction in a large Barge presented themselves with splendid Colors, Boat after Boat & Sloop after Sloop added to our little fleet gaily dressed with every naval Armament —we began to mak a most elegant appearance. Before we got to Bedlars Island a large Sloop. came. with full sail on our Starboard Bow, when about 20 Gentn & Ladies rose up. and with excellent & melodious Voices sung an Eloquent Ode appropriate to the occasion. & set to the Music of "God save the King," welcoming their Great Chief to the Seat of Government. At the conclusion we gave them our Hats, and then they with the surrounding Boats., gave three Hurra's which made the neighboring shores rebound with the Joyful acclamation Soon after another Boat came under our Stern and threw in amongst us a number of Copies of another Ode. and immediately about a dozen Gentn began to sing it in parts as we passed along. Our Worthy President was greatly affected with these tokens of profound respect & gratitude.

As we approached the Harbour Our Train increased and the Hurraing & Shouts of Joy added great vivacity to this lively scene. At this moment a shoal of porpoises came rising above the water & playing among the Boats. as if desirous to know the Cause of all this Joy & Gladness.—We now discovered the Shores crowded with thousands of People. Men Women & Children. Nay I may.

venture to say. Tens of Thousands, from the Battery
to the place of Landing Altho) nearly half a Mile
you could see little else along the Wharves in the
Streets. and on board the Vessels, but heads as
numerous as Ears of Corn before the Harvest. The
Vessels in the Harbour presented a most superb
appearance draped in all the pomp of national Gaity
& Elegance A Spanish Packett. then lying in the
Harbour in a Moment on a signal given hoisted 27
or 28 different Colors of All Nations on every part
of the Rigging and paid a compliment of 13 Guns
with all her Yards maned. as did another Vessel in
the Harbour displaying colors in like manner.
From the Battery we had the like compliment of
18 Pounders.

We soon arrived at the Ferry Stairs in Wall
Street where many thousands of the Citizens and a
chosen detachment of the Militia in Elegant Uniform, waiting with all eagerness of Expectation,
welcomed this most excellent man. to that Shore.
which he had by his Judgment, & Courageous per-
severance regained from a powerful Enemy almost
against Hope. We found the Stairs Covered with
Carpeting, and the rails from the Water to the top
of the warf hung with crimson hangings. The
president being preceeded by the committee, was
received by the Govenor and the principal Citizens
in the most brilliant and affectionate manner, he
was met on the warf by many of his old and faithful companions and fellow patriots who had with

him borne the heat & burthen of the day, and
who like him had experienced every reverse of
fortune with fortitude and patience & who now
Joined the universal chorus of welcome to the
Great deliverer (under providence) from all their
fears, It was with difficulty a passage could be
made by the troops through the pressing crowd,
who seemed incapable of being satisfied in gazing
at this man of the people, You will see the particulars of the procession from the wharf to the
house appointed for the presidents residence in the
newspaper, The streets were lined with inhabitants
as close as they could stand together, and it
required all the exertions of a numerous train of
City officers with their staves to make a passage for
the procession. The houses were filled with Gents
& Ladies elegantly dressed, and the whole distance
being about half a mile & the windows to the highest stories were illuminated by the Sparkling eyes
of innumerable companies of Ladies who seemed
to vie with each other to show the Joy on this great
occasion It was full half an hour before we could
finish our commission, by introducing our Charge
into the house prepared by order of Congress for
his reception as soon as this was done, not withstanding the presidents great fatigue both of body
& mind, he had to receive the Gentlemen of Congress, & the City, the Officers of the Army and
Militia, forming a very numerous body, all of whom
were eagerly desirous to show their respect in the

most affectionate manner, This duty he performed with great ease and that friendly and obliging demeanor he was so famous for—When this was finished and the people dispersed we went undressed, and dined with his excellency Gov. Clinton who had provided an elegant dinner for the purpose—thus ended our Commission—The evening though very wet (having rained to-wards night) was spent by all ranks in visiting from street to street, the whole City being illuminated in a very pleasing manner—I cannot help taking notice how highly we were favored in the providential disposition of the weather, the whole procession being completely finished, and we had repaired to the Governours before the Gust arose——When the president was on the wharf. an officer came up politely addressing him, said he had the honor and peculiar felicity of commanding his Guard, and was ready to obey his orders The president much affected answered, that as to any present arrangement he desired that it might be carried into execution agreable to orders but afterwards he hoped the officer would give himself no further trouble, as the affections of his fellow Citizens (turning to the thousands around him) were all the Guard he wanted.

The General was conveyed from Elizabeth town in an elegant barge built for the purpose and rowed by 12 old Captains of Vessels who had retired from business, and now had become reputable and wealthy Citizens of New York. They were dressed in White shirts adorned with ribbons The Committee was on the barge with the General and his suite.

The Committee were

Of the Senate $\left\{\begin{array}{l}\text{MR LANGDON} \\ \text{MR ———} \\ \text{MR ———}\end{array}\right.$

House of Representatives $\left\{\begin{array}{l}\text{MR BOUDINOT} \\ \text{MR BLAND} \\ \text{MR TUCKER} \\ \text{MR BENSON} \\ \text{MR LAURENCE}\end{array}\right.$

Troops furnished by each state during the Revolutionary War, 1776 to 1784.

STATE.	POPULATION 1782.	TROOPS FURNISHED	PROPORTION
New Hampshire . .	100,000	14,000	1-7th
Massachusetts . . .	390,000	83,000	1-5th
Connecticut	208,000	40,000	1-5th
Rhode Island . . .	50,000	10,000	1-5th
New York	236,000	21,000	1-11th
New Jersey	140,000	17,000	1-8th
Pennsylvania . . .	380,000	32,000	1-12th
Delaware			
North Carolina . . .	250,000	7,000	1-33d
South Carolina . . .	100,000	6,000	1-16th
Georgia	70,000	2,600	1-25th
Virginia			
Maryland			
	1,918,000	232,600	Averages 1-8th

FINIS.

Com-
mittee whilst abroad with Ribbons   The Committee was on the barge with the General and his
suite.

The Committee were

Of the Senate { MR ——————
                MR ——————
                MR LANGDON }

House of Representatives { MR LAURENCE
                           MR BENSON
                           MR TUCKER
                           MR BLAND
                           MR BOUDINOT }

Troops furnished by each state during the Revolutionary War, 1775 to 1783.

STATE.	POPULATION.	TROOPS FUR-NISHED	PROPORTION
New Hampshire	100,000	14,000	1-7th
Massachusetts	360,000	83,000	1 2th
Connecticut	208,000	40,000	1-5th
Rhode Island	50,000	10,000	1-5th
New York	238,000	21,000	1-11th
New Jersey	140,000	17,000	1-8th
Pennsylvania	380,000	32,000	1-12th
Delaware			
North Carolina	250,000	7,000	1-33d
South Carolina	100,000	6,000	1-16th
Georgia	70,000	2,600	1-25th
Virginia			
Maryland			
	1,918,000	332,600	Averages 1-8th